AMERICAN HORTICULTURAL SOCIETY
PRACTICAL GUIDES

PLANTS FROM
CUTTINGS

AMERICAN HORTICULTURAL SOCIETY
PRACTICAL GUIDES

PLANTS FROM
CUTTINGS

ALAN TOOGOOD

DK Publishing

LONDON, NEW YORK, MUNICH, MELBOURNE, and DELHI

PROJECT EDITOR Fiona Wild
ART EDITOR Colin Walton
US EDITOR Ray Rogers

SERIES EDITOR Helen Fewster
SERIES ART EDITOR Ursula Dawson

MANAGING EDITOR Anna Kruger
MANAGING ART EDITOR Lee Griffiths

DTP DESIGNER Louise Waller
PRODUCTION MANAGER Mandy Inness

First American Edition, 2003
00 01 02 03 04 05 10 9 8 7 6 5 4 3 2 1

Published in the United States by
DK Publishing, Inc.
375 Hudson Street
New York, NY 10014

Library of Congress Cataloging-in-Publication data is available
from the Library of Congress
ISBN 0-7894-9296-2

Reproduced by Colourscan, Singapore
Printed and bound by Star Standard Industries, Singapore

See our complete catalog at
www.dk.com

CONTENTS

PLANTS GROWN FROM CUTTINGS 7
An introduction to growing plants from cuttings:
the history and the different techniques.

RAISING PLANTS FROM CUTTINGS 23
TOOLS AND SUNDRIES 24
ROOTING MEDIA 26
PREPARING CUTTINGS 28
TYPES OF CUTTING 30

CARING FOR CUTTINGS 49
PROPAGATING UNDER COVER 49
CLOCHES AND COLD FRAMES 52
CARE OF CUTTINGS UNDER COVER 54
THE ROOTED CUTTINGS 56
CUTTINGS IN THE OPEN 58

PLANTS TO GROW FROM CUTTINGS 61
GARDEN TREES 61
SHRUBS AND CLIMBERS 64
PERENNIALS 69
CACTI AND SUCCULENTS 76

Index 78
Acknowledgments 80

PLANTS GROWN FROM CUTTINGS

WHY GROW PLANTS FROM CUTTINGS?

PLANTS HAVE EVOLVED A FASCINATING ARRAY of strategies in order to survive and increase, and since the dawn of civilization, farmers and gardeners have used their observations to develop propagation methods in cultivation. Raising new plants from cuttings is often a straightforward process, and today it is possible for everyone to make the most of the known techniques, from the child with a jar of water to the nurseryman with heated greenhouses.

EXPLOITING NATURE

Propagation from cuttings began when rooted shoots or suckers were detached and replanted. This led to propagation from unrooted shoots. The great advantage of propagating plant material in this way is that the new plant is genetically identical to the parent. If you need large numbers of plants, for example tender perennials for bedding, then preparing trays of cuttings will be a much more economical method of increasing your stock than buying from a nursery or garden center. Another plus is that if you admire a plant in a friend's or neighbor's garden, it is often possible to re-create it in your own by taking a few cuttings and caring for them well, and without damage to the parent plant.

CLEMATIS 'PERLE D'AZUR'
This deciduous climber can be propagated in various ways. Leaf-bud cuttings, for example, should be taken from softwood and semi-ripe shoots. It will take 2–3 years for the new plants to flower.

◀ PLANTS FOR FREE *Many geraniums and fuchsias are easily grown from cuttings.*

ADAPTING FROM NATURE

P ROPAGATION, AND GARDENING GENERALLY, is easier if plants are suitable for the climate and can be grown outdoors all year round. Plants that are grown outside their natural habitats generally require artificially enhanced conditions under cover, such as heat and humidity, for propagation. Success in propagation usually depends on providing a supportive environment for the plant material and, later, the new plants. Understanding how plants function will help, too.

SURVIVAL IN THE WILD

Plants are amazingly capable of survival and can increase in all kinds of conditions. They have adapted to a wide range of adverse habitats, such as deserts (cacti), high altitudes where winds damage foliage and discourage pollinating insects (alpines), and water (aquatics) where the problems are different yet again.

All flowering plants reproduce by seeds (sexual reproduction) or by vegetative (asexual) methods. Nature has overcome the limitations of seeds by adopting asexual reproduction, producing offspring (clones) that are genetically identical to the parent.

Plants have many ways of increasing vegetatively from modified roots or stems. The simplest way they do this is by forming a closely knit mass (crown) of shoots and buds, each of which is capable of becoming a separate plant.

Some plants can regenerate shoots or roots from growth tissue to produce new plants (runners or layers). Others form

---

Cuttings are one way to exploit natural regenerative processes

---

special food-storing organs, including stem tubers (potatoes), corms (crocuses), and pseudobulbs (orchids). This enables a plant to survive a hostile situation, saving energy for more favorable conditions.

KEEPING WARM
An artificial environment has been created for these ivy cuttings by draping opaque plastic film over hoops on a heated bench to increase warmth and humidity around the cuttings. Both factors aid rooting.

Gardeners have adapted natural vegetative, or clonal, reproduction to obtain plants that are always "true" to the parent. Cuttings are one artificial way to increase plants by exploiting their regenerative abilities. Clonal propagation does carry its own dangers, however, since genetically identical plants carry the same susceptibility to disease.

Gardeners can choose a propagation method to meet both their needs and the capacity of each plant to reproduce in the local conditions. Knowing the plant family can be a useful guide to rooting cuttings successfully. For example, most plants in the Gesneriaceae, such as African violets (*Saintpaulia*), *Columnea*, *Ramonda*, and *Streptocarpus*, readily regenerate from leaf tissue. The Menthaceae, including *Salvia* (sage), *Solenostemon* (coleus), *Lamium*, and rosemary, root easily from stem cuttings – in the wild, stems close to moist soil often produce roots.

Another factor is the plant's natural limit of distribution; often reproductive ability declines outside this area. This may be countered by providing controlled conditions for propagation.

WHICH PART OF THE PLANT?

Most cuttings are taken from the plant stem, and in many cases several cuttings can be taken from one long length of a plant's new season's growth. They can vary in degree of ripeness (maturity) from unripe (softwood cuttings) to fully ripe (hardwood cuttings). Cuttings may also be taken from leaves or roots. A few plants can regenerate from a detached leaf or section of leaf tissue. These include members of the families Begoniaceae, Crassulaceae, and Gesneriaceae. It is possible to root leaves of plants such as *Clematis*, *Hoya*, and *Mahonia*, but leaf cuttings of these cannot produce buds and so can never develop into plants. Some plants, such as acanthus, can be propagated from root cuttings.

STEM CUTTING
Stems are used to prepare cuttings of many plants. The current year's growth is selected: it may be soft (as in the hydrangea cuttings shown here), partially ripe, or fully ripe.

PART-LEAF CUTTING
A few plants, such as the begonia shown here, regenerate from leaf tissue. Take leaf sections or wound leaves at any time in the growing season.

ROOT CUTTING
Lengths of healthy, strong root can be taken (here from an acanthus) in the dormant season of pencil or medium thickness for the plant.

CUTTINGS IN THE PAST

T HE CULTIVATION AND PROPAGATION OF PLANTS began when human tribes
abandoned their nomadic, hunter-gatherer way of life to live in settled
communities. This change occurred just after the last Ice Age and marked the
beginning of modern civilization. The development of bread wheat triggered the
advent of agricultural practices, and alongside developed techniques for raising
plants from seeds and cuttings, as well as grafting rootstocks and layering.

ORIGINS OF PROPAGATION

Ancient civilizations throughout the world
grew a wide range of food crops after
noting how plants naturally dispersed seeds
that later produced seedlings. In ancient
Greek and Roman times, writers such as
the poet Virgil recorded current methods of
propagation in some detail. Olives, date
palms, and cypresses were grown from
seeds as well as other food plants, such
as cabbages, turnips, lettuces, and herbs.
Propagation from cuttings began when

The Romans dipped
the bases of cuttings
in ox manure

---

rooted shoots or suckers were detached
from the parent plant and replanted, and
this led to propagation from unrooted
shoots. Romans dipped the bases of
cuttings in ox manure to stimulate rooting.

In the Middle Ages, settlers discovered
how to propagate superior forms of grapes,
olives, and figs to preserve their desirable
characteristics by thrusting woody stems
into the soil.

By 2000 BC, grafting was fairly common
in Greece, the Middle East, Egypt, and
China. Grafting was used to propagate
plants that were difficult to root from
cuttings and to encourage early fruiting.

Other natural vegetative-reproduction
methods were exploited by propagating
from food-storage organs such as bulbs,

AARON'S ROD
*The Bible story of Aaron's rod, a stave that
"brought forth buds, and bloomed blossoms
and yielded almonds," is in effect a
description of an early hardwood cutting.*

tubers, and rhizomes. Toward the dawn of
the first century AD, plant propagation
practices were already well established.

THE VICTORIANS

An explosion of plant-hunting took place
in the western world in the 18th and 19th
centuries. A wealth of new and exciting
plants were discovered and traded between
Europe and Japan, China, India, the East
Indies, Australasia, Africa, and North and
South America. New introductions arrived
as seeds, bulbs, or whole plants.

Enthusiasm for these new plants and the desire to grow and propagate them, coupled with the financial wealth of the plant collectors' patrons, was the inspiration for the golden age of the greenhouse. The Victorians were highly inventive in greenhouse construction and design, and their methods of controlling temperature, light, and humidity in the greenhouses were impressively complex. Techniques became more refined and propagation techniques increasingly creative, even if trial and error must have been used when attempting to increase stocks of each unfamiliar plant.

Their propagation equipment was fairly basic, yet the ideas of the Victorians form the foundation of techniques used today.

To control temperature and humidity, they built cold frames and hot beds. Cold frames, sited to capture as much warmth as possible from the sun, especially in winter, were used for root cuttings, easy stem cuttings, and seeds. Hot beds consisted of a glazed frame set in a pit, filled with equal parts fresh manure and deciduous leaves, a mix that generated heat for up to eight weeks after being mixed and turned.

Bell jars were also used in great numbers. These bell-shaped glass jars were placed over cuttings in prepared soil or in pots, and warmth was provided by solar radiation. Although difficult to control precisely, it was possible to maintain high humidity inside the jars. Today, bell jars have largely been replaced by more versatile covers.

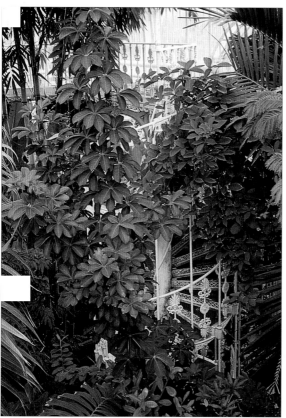

◄ THE PALM HOUSE AT KEW
Heated greenhouses like the Palm House at the Royal Botanic Gardens Kew enabled Victorian gardeners to grow many tropical plants.

▼ VICTORIAN HOT BED
Victorian gardeners often made use of hot beds for propagation and for raising exotic vegetables or fruits, such as pineapples.

MODERN PROPAGATION TECHNIQUES

THE PROPAGATION EQUIPMENT that was available to Victorian gardeners was fairly primitive compared with modern advances, yet their ideas still form the basis of what is done today. Since the 1950s, modern technology and increased collaboration and information exchange among professionals has led to the development of new propagation techniques for the first time in centuries. These new methods make propagation much easier today.

MIST AND FOG PROPAGATION

A unit known as the intermittent mist propagation system was devised in the 1950s for rooting stem cuttings, in particular softwood and semi-ripe material (*see pp.30–35*). Cables along the base of the unit provide bottom heat, stimulating rooting, and constantly regulated humidity keeps the cuttings cool and moist. A soil thermostat regulates the temperature of the sand or bed of medium. The advance meant that many plants that had previously been grafted could now be rooted at a fraction of the cost. Mist propagation is widely used in commercial propagation and is useful for gardeners. If a dedicated unit is beyond your means, you can create your own using soil-warming cables and a misting system in a closed case.

With fog propagation, a much smaller water droplet is created than with mist propagation, creating conditions in which the air remains moist for a much longer period. The foliage is not heavily moistened, making this a good technique for cuttings that are prone to rot.

PLASTIC FILM

Another development of the 1950s was plastic film. An effective propagation environment can be created using a unit with bottom heat, plus plastic film (a sheet of opaque plastic) mounted over the top.

Use plastic film to warm soil in a cold frame before use

The cover creates a high-humidity environment around the tops of the cuttings. Plastic film can also be used with cold frames to warm soil before cuttings are inserted and then to cover new plants in the frame.

PROPAGATING BLANKET
This specialized blanket is made of electric wires encased in aluminum foil to provide an even distribution of heat. The blanket may be used on a greenhouse bench or on the floor to provide a temporary propagation area for plant material in pots or in unheated propagators. When not in use, it may be rolled up and stored.

Thermostat can be set to required temperature

Probe monitors temperature at surface

Propagator

Capillary matting

Plastic sheet protects blanket

Electric blanket

Polystyrene insulation pad

Greenhouse bench

Misting head sprays fine droplets

Heated propagating bench

Hood fitted with grow lamps

Thermostat | Water reservoir

MIST PROPAGATION UNIT
The misting head sprays fine droplets over the cuttings, cooling the top-growth and retaining moisture. The heated bench aids rooting.

FOG PROPAGATION UNIT
Fresh air is pumped through a water reservoir, creating a warm fog around the cuttings. Vapor condenses at the sides and runs back.

MICROPROPAGATION

The technique of micropropagation, used to raise huge numbers of plants from a small amount of material, was developed in the 1960s. New cultivars, virus-free crop plants such as raspberries, and plants that are difficult to propagate by traditional means can be propagated in quantity in this way. It is also a very useful way of increasing old and rare plants from existing stocks to conserve plants in the wild. This is a commercial technique only, but the end results are of benefit to gardeners.

Micropropagation usually involves growing pieces of plant tissue *in vitro* in sterile laboratory conditions. Most plants are able to regenerate from a single cell. Tissue from the shoot tip (meristem) is most commonly used, but root tips, calluses (which form on wounds), anthers, flower buds, leaves, seeds, or fruits may also provide suitable tissue. In specially adapted growing rooms, temperature, light levels, nutrients, and hormones are regulated. The resulting plants are then grown on in greenhouse conditions.

Viruses and systemic disease rarely penetrate growing tips, so micropropagated plants are normally disease-free and therefore may be safely introduced to other countries.

Although micropropagation is capable of producing large quantities of plants, it is still an expensive procedure. Another disadvantage is that plants may fail to adapt to a normal growing environment.

CULTURED PLANT TISSUE
Plant cells (here of tobacco, Nicotiana) are grown on a nutrient gel until the cell mass produces embryo plants.

LEAF CUTTING
Plantlets can be grown from a tiny leaf cutting, as with these African violets. In sterile conditions, better yields can be obtained.

REGENERATION

THE PROCESS OF TAKING CUTTINGS is relatively simple in most cases, but success will depend on several factors. The inherent ability of the parent plant to produce roots will determine the degree of care needed to coax cuttings to root. Also, the condition of the parent influences the quality of the rooted cutting. Always choose a healthy plant; diseases or pests can be transmitted to a cutting. Good hygiene is essential to avoid introducing disease.

SUCCESS WITH CUTTINGS

Plants have a remarkable ability to regenerate themselves from little more than a piece of the stem, leaf, root, or a bud into a fully developed plant with a root system and shoots. Vegetative propagation exploits this natural ability and extends it.

To produce these roots, a group of growth cells (known as the meristem), which are usually close to the central core of vascular (sap-carrying) tissue, change into root cells. These then form root buds and then adventitious roots. These are also called "induced" or "wound" roots because, in most plants, they occur only after wounding, such as when a piece of stem is cut off to produce a cutting.

In some plants, preformed root initials lie dormant in the stems, so they root rapidly and easily from cuttings. A few plants even form root buds, normally visible at the bases of shoots. Other, often hardy, woody plants are difficult to root; with these, callusing may hinder root formation, and grafting may be necessary. In warm climates, cuttings of many plants may be rooted outdoors, directly inserted into prepared soil in shade, at almost any

◄ CLINGING IVY
*Ivies (*Hedera*) develop stem roots, known as adventitious roots, that cling to vertical surfaces.*

▲ IVY ROOTS
The stem roots are clearly visible against the wall. These evergreen climbers root readily in the wild.

time of year. In cooler areas, a controlled environment is often vital; rooting may be unpredictable and slow. Bottom heat of 59–77°F (15–25°C) can promote rooting. The air should be much cooler than the growing medium to avoid encouraging growth of foliage instead of roots. The rooting medium should be moist and (for leafy cuttings) the air kept humid.

The time taken for a cutting to root depends on the plant, the type of cutting, the age of the stem, how it was prepared,

> A piece of leaf may have the ability to grow into a fully developed plant

and the rooting environment. Leafy cuttings, particularly softwood and greenwood cuttings of woody plants and perennials (including basal cuttings), may root in about three weeks; woody cuttings from trees and shrubs may take up to five months. The new plants are genetically identical to the parent, and characteristics such as variegated leaves can be preserved.

CALLUSING
When a stem is cut or wounded, it forms callus tissue (see inset) over the damaged cells. In difficult-to-root plants, or if the medium is too aerated or alkaline (high pH), the callus pad may thicken, preventing root growth. If this happens, pare away the excess.

NODAL CUTTING
The cells involved in growth are most concentrated at the nodes, or leaf joints, so most cuttings are trimmed just below a node to optimize root formation.

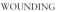

Use a clean, sharp knife

WOUNDING
A cutting from semi-ripe or hard wood often roots more readily if bark is cut away from the base of the stem. This exposes more of the growth cells in the cambium layer.

1in (2.5cm) cut exposes growth cells

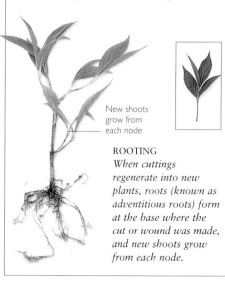

New shoots grow from each node

ROOTING
When cuttings regenerate into new plants, roots (known as adventitious roots) form at the base where the cut or wound was made, and new shoots grow from each node.

HEEL CUTTING
Some cuttings, especially of semi-ripe wood, are taken by pulling away a small sideshoot so that it retains a "heel" of bark from the main shoot.

Heel contains high levels of growth hormone

WOODY PLANTS

T REES, SHRUBS, CONIFERS, AND WOODY CLIMBERS form the backbone of any garden planting but vary enormously in habit, form, and productive lifespan. They can be propagated by an equally wide range of techniques, but taking cuttings is one of the most common propagation methods, especially where a large number of new plants is desired (for example, for a hedge). It is usually a fairly simple process and provides new plants relatively quickly.

SHRUBS AND WOODY CLIMBERS

Shrubs and climbing plants represent an invaluable and long-lasting source of shape, texture, and color in the garden. A shrub is a deciduous or evergreen perennial with multiple woody stems or branches, generally originating from or near its base. Subshrubs are woody-based plants with soft-wooded stems. Climbers are plants that climb or cling by means of modified stems,

> The majority of shrubs and climbers are best propagated by cuttings

roots, leaves, or leaf-stalks, using other plants or objects as support.

Choosing the type of cutting, and the maturity of the wood, is very important to the success of the propagation process.

It is important to select cutting material very carefully, avoiding any shoots where pests or diseases may be present and discarding any damaged material. Cuttings root most easily when the parent plant is young and producing good lengths of new growth each year. Most cuttings are best taken from the current season's growth.

HONEYSUCKLE
Climbing honeysuckles, such as this Lonicera periclymenum *'Serotina', are easily propagated from different types of growth: softwood, semi-ripe, or hardwood cuttings taken from late spring to winter.*

The cuttings of some shrubs, such as deciduous azaleas and magnolias, root best if the material is forced into early growth under protection early in the year.

GARDEN TREES

Trees may provide the framework or focal point of a garden and can also link the garden with the landscape beyond. They are woody perennials with a crown of branches, usually at the top of a single stem or trunk and include conifers, or cone-bearing trees. Valued for their shape, which provides year-round interest, many trees also offer seasonal displays of handsome foliage as well as bark, flowers, and colorful fruit. Since trees are slow-growing compared with herbaceous plants, they can be expensive, so it is worth propagating your own, especially if a number of plants are needed for hedges, woodland gardens, or screening. Propagating also makes it possible to increase unusual species or to replace old trees.

Some hardwood cuttings will yield a sapling ready for planting out in the open in one year; other types of cutting will need to be grown on for two to three years. However, a few plants, *Nothofagus* for example, can take up to five years.

▶ HOLLY
Variegated hollies like this Ilex aquifolium *'Ovata Aurea' keep their coloring when grown from cuttings. Semi-ripe cuttings of this readily rooting holly can be taken fom late summer onward.*

▲ CAMELLIA
This Camellia × williamsii *'E.G. Waterhouse' could be increased by taking semi-ripe cuttings from midsummer on.*

▶ CONIFER
Chamaecyparis lawsoniana *'Minima Aurea' can be grown from semi-ripe cuttings taken in late summer or autumn.*

PERENNIALS

THIS HUGELY VARIED GROUP OF PLANTS encompasses not only traditional border herbaceous perennials but also alpines, water garden plants, orchids, and tender plants for summer bedding and greenhouse display. Many perennials are easily propagated from cuttings, enabling the gardener to keep existing plants healthy and vigorous, replace short-lived perennials as they die, and build up stocks for an effective border display.

MAINTAINING THE LINE

The majority of perennials make new growth from the base or crown; their roots or rhizomes spread, and the plants naturally form clumps. To give impact to plantings, perennials are often required in quantity – cuttings provide the means. They also provide the best way of obtaining plants that are true to the parent with all their special characteristics such as blooms of a particular color, or large or double flowers. This also applies to plants bred not to flower, such as the lawn chamomile 'Treneague'; foliage plants with finely cut, differently colored, or variegated leaves; single-sex plants; and sterile hybrids.

TYPES OF CUTTINGS

A wide range of perennials can be raised from cuttings, using a variety of plant parts – stems, leaves, and roots. In most cases, some form of controlled environment – a heated propagator, greenhouse, or cold frame – is necessary to encourage cuttings to generate missing parts such as roots. If these conditions can be provided, cuttings are ideal for obtaining a number of new perennials that will be ready to plant out, and may even flower, in their second year.

Mature plants recover well from having a modest amount of cutting material removed. Stock plants can be cultivated especially for the purpose of providing cuttings. They should be compact and bushy, with lots of young shoots.

TIMING

With some perennials, you can take cuttings at almost any time of the year they are not in flower. With others, material is suitable only during a few weeks or even days. If taken after flowering, many cuttings will root and grow well. Cuttings from perennials that die down over winter should be taken early in the growing season to give them a long growing period.

OENOTHERA MACROCARPA
Ozark sundrops may be easily propagated from softwood tip cuttings or basal stem cuttings taken in the spring.

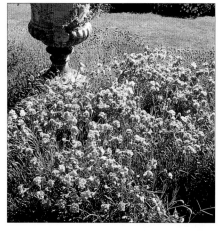

▲ ANEMONE
To avoid disturbing
Japanese anemones
like this Anemone ×
hybrida 'Max Vogel',
uncover the edge of
the clump to take
root cuttings.

▶ PINKS
Semi-ripe cuttings, or
"pipings," may be
taken from all pinks
(Dianthus), especially
small and alpine
species. Plants should
flower the next year.

▲ MINT
Take rhizome
cuttings of mint (here
Mentha suaveolens
'Variegata') in spring,
then root with bottom
heat of 50°F (10°C).

▼ DRUMSTICK
PRIMROSE
Root cuttings can be
used to propagate
Primula denticulata
and its color forms.
Cut thicker roots of
the parent plant into
pieces (see p.44).

CACTI AND OTHER SUCCULENTS

SUCCULENTS EVOLVED TO SURVIVE in habitats with extreme conditions, particularly periods of drought. The sculptural forms of this extraordinary group of plants belie the comparative ease with which many of those in popular cultivation may be propagated. Cacti all belong to one family of stem succulents, distinguished by the areole, a padlike bud from which flowers, shoots, and spines grow. Other succulents span many plant families.

DIVERSITY OF FORMS

Succulents store water in specialized tissue in swollen roots, stems, or leaves. Many desert species have tiny leaves (or none at all) in order to retain moisture and withstand drought. Others are rainforest epiphytes, living in trees and absorbing water through straplike stems. Other succulents are very diverse in form, from stark, cactuslike barrels to treelike leafy species, and they are also diverse in the ways they may be propagated. Some techniques, such as stem and leaf cuttings, are broadly similar to those used on herbaceous perennials, but with the advantage that succulent cuttings do not wilt as quickly. However, fleshy cuttings are very susceptible to rot, so good hygiene is essential for successful propagation of these plants.

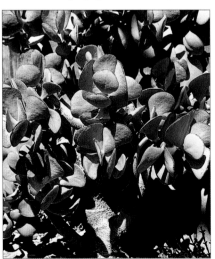

Some cacti and other succulents do not flower readily in cultivation, and commercial seeds are often not readily available, so taking cuttings offers a reliable way of increasing many of these plants. Succulent cuttings have the advantage that, because of their fleshy tissue, they can retain nutrients and water while they become established.

Unusual forms, such as variegated, monstrose, or cristate (crested) plants, plus hybrids, can usually be propagated only from cuttings (or by grafting) to preserve their distinctive characteristics.

TYPES OF CUTTING

There are various types of cuttings, and the most suitable technique depends on the plant's form and growth habit. Succulents are generally propagated by stem, leaf, or rosette cuttings, while cacti are raised from globular, columnar, or flat stem cuttings. Many clump-forming species produce unrooted offsets that may also be treated as cuttings.

The best time to take cuttings of most succulents, especially in cooler climates, is in late spring or early summer, when the warmer, drier weather arrives and the plants have started to grow strongly. It then gives them a chance to establish for as long as possible before the following winter.

CRASSULA
In the wild, crassula leaves that have fallen on the ground often take root. Crassula arborescens, the silver jade plant, shown here, can be rooted from semi-ripe stem cuttings.

▲ SUCCULENTS
Cuttings offer a reliable way of increasing succulents, since they retain water while rooting.

▶ CACTI
Offsets taken from cacti like Mammillaria zeilmanniana *may be treated in the same way as stem cuttings.*

◀ ORCHID CACTUS
The orchid cactus, Epiphyllum crenatum, *can be easily propagated from flat stem cuttings taken from spring to late summer. The cuttings should root in 3–6 weeks.*

RAISING PLANTS FROM CUTTINGS

CHOOSING AND GATHERING

THE FIRST PRINCIPLE OF PROPAGATION is to take material from healthy, strong plants, because pests and diseases can be transmitted from the parent. Look for clean, vigorous growth, avoiding weak or very spindly shoots, and make sure that your standards of hygiene are high. Choosing the type of cutting (and the maturity of the material) best suited to a particular plant is very important to the success of the propagation process.

UNDERSTANDING THE BASICS

Cuttings from trees, shrubs, and woody climbers root most easily when the parent plant is young and producing good lengths of new growth each year. Most cuttings will be from wood of the current season's growth. Some shrubs, such as deciduous azaleas and magnolias, generally root best if the material is forced under protection early in the year.

Stem cuttings from perennials that die down over winter should be taken early on in the growing season, so that the cuttings have plenty of time to form good root systems. They will need these to come through the next dormant phase.

Hardwood cuttings from woody plants should be taken during the dormant period, usually from mid- to late autumn through late winter. Softwood cuttings are usually taken in late spring from the fast-growing tips of new shoots. Semi-ripe cuttings are taken during the summer.

Always use very clean, sharp cutting tools, and never allow cuttings to dry out, either when preparing them or when growing on.

CUTTINGS FROM STOCK PLANTS

A stock plant is grown purely to provide cutting material and can be encouraged to produce the best type of growth for this purpose. A stock plant should be healthy, mature, and vigorous, with compact, bushy growth and lots of young shoots. It should be a good example of its type and flower and fruit well. No more than 60 percent of the top-growth should be taken from a stock plant at any one time.

REGULAR SUPPLY
A container-grown plant can supply cuttings repeatedly. This hebe yielded 84 cuttings without its shape being spoiled.

◀ PLANTS TO PROPAGATE *Honeysuckle, broom, and hebe are all easily raised from cuttings.*

TOOLS AND SUNDRIES

A N ASSORTMENT OF ITEMS will prove either useful or essential in the preparation of propagating material, from basics such as garden knives and pots to specialized propagators. A small but essential item is the label: always label propagation trays to avoid confusion later. When preparing to take cuttings, it is important to use the most appropriate knife. Dibbers are handy for making planting holes, and widgers are useful for lifting delicate cuttings.

KNIVES AND CUTTERS

Use a garden or budding knife with a plastic or wooden handle for softwood or semi-ripe cuttings. Most have a carbon steel blade that folds into the handle. Use a scalpel or fine-bladed craft knife for very small cuttings and for cutting soft tissue such as succulents. Pruners are good for woody cuttings.

▲ PRUNERS
Pruners are used to prepare woody material, such as hardwood cuttings. Bypass pruners, shown here, are better than anvil types, since they do not bruise the stems.

◄ SHARPENING STONE
Use this to keep the blades of knives and pruners sharp. A sharp blade will not crush delicate plant tissue.

LABELING

Plastic labels (*below*) are widely used when propagating plants from cuttings. They may be written on in pencil so are reusable, although writing does fade and the plastic becomes brittle over time.

| GARDEN KNIFE | BUDDING KNIFE | SCALPEL | STEEL WIDGER | PLASTIC WIDGER | SMALL DIBBER |

PLANT POTS

A wide range of containers, including the traditional pot and seed tray, is available for propagation purposes. Plastic is more hygienic, lighter, and cheaper than clay or terracotta. Plastic pots also retain more moisture, although clay pots offer better aeration and drainage and are a good choice for alpines. Flexible plastic and soft plastic pots are cheaper than rigid pots but are generally used only once.

POTS FOR PROPAGATION
An assortment of sizes will be needed. The most useful are the 3½ in (9cm) and 5in (12.5cm).

CELL TRAYS

Cell (or module) trays have been used commercially for a number of years and are now widely available to the amateur gardener. The cells allow cuttings to develop sturdy root systems before being potted up. The cells also mean the young plants can be handled without disturbing roots or harming the stems. Care is needed in watering, because the trays can dry out quickly. Trays in a range of sizes are now available for propagation purposes; a 1½in (37mm) cell tray is the most approp-riate size for small herbaccous cuttings.

Trays of rockwool units (a porous material made from fibers spun from molten mineral rock) can also be used, but the cuttings will need to be fertilized with a dilute liquid fertilizer as soon as they have rooted and periodically if they remain in the rockwool for a while. Standard or half seed trays may also be used for rooting all kinds of cuttings.

▲ TRAYS AND INSERTS
Trays made of plastic fit into a standard seed tray. Drip trays with capillary matting allow watering from below.

▶ CELL TRAYS
These cell, or module, trays in a range of sizes allow rooted cuttings to be potted without too much root disturbance.

THE IMPORTANCE OF HYGIENE

It is essential to maintain high standards of hygiene when propagating plants in order to prevent any possible contamination by pests and diseases. Sterilize tools and equipment before use, either by heating them or wiping them in rubbing alcohol before each cut. Dirty containers can harbor minute pests; make sure they are throughly scrubbed, rinsed, and dried before use. Close-fitting latex gloves are ideal for use when propagating. They are sterile and also protect your skin against irritant sap.

RUBBER GLOVES

STERILIZING KNIVES
To sterilize a knife, dip the blade in rubbing alcohol and pass it quickly through a flame.

WASHING POTS
Thoroughly scrub dirty pots using a stiff brush dipped in dilute horticultural disinfectant. Rinse well.

ROOTING MEDIA

THE RIGHT ROOTING MEDIUM is crucial to success with cuttings. Soil beds outdoors are often used for hardwood cuttings, but most cuttings need soilless mixes or other media under cover. You can mix your own medium to obtain the ideal one for individual plants. Most rooting media are based on peat or peat substitutes combined with other ingredients with different properties. Sterile, inert substances such as perlite and vermiculite are useful.

COMMON INGREDIENTS FOR MEDIA

When rooting cuttings under cover, peat is usually preferred to soil, because it is light, well aerated, and relatively free from pests and diseases. Media intended for rooting cuttings need to be freely draining. A standard rooting medium typically contains equal parts of sand and peat substitute (or peat). It may also be based on bark or perlite or a high proportion of coarse sand (not beach sand). Media like these are low in nutrients, so the cuttings will need to be fertilized once rooted. Alternatively, for cuttings that will be in the pot for some time, such as those for woody plants, add a little fertilizer to the bottom of the pot so that the new roots will not be scorched.

LOAM
High-quality, sterilized soil with good nutrient supply, drainage, aeration, and moisture retention. For soilbased media.

GRIT
Used in very fine (2–3mm) or fine (5mm) to coarse (7–12mm) grades. Aids drainage for alpines and cacti.

PEAT
Stable, long-lasting, well aerated, and moisture-retentive, but low in nutrients. For lightweight, short-term media.

PERLITE
Expanded volcanic rock granules. Sterile, inert, and light; retains moisture but drains freely. Medium/coarse grades aid aeration.

FINE BARK
Fine grades of chipped pine bark used as a peat substitute or for very freely draining, acidic media good for rooting cuttings.

VERMICULITE
Expanded and airblown mica. Acts in a similar way to perlite but holds more water and less air. Fine grade aids drainage.

COIR
Fiber from coconut husks, used as peat substitute. Dries out less quickly than peat but needs fertilizer. Base for soilless mix.

SAND
Fine sand (left) helps promote drainage and aeration; coarse sand (right) gives more open texture to rooting media.

LEAF MOLD
Well-rotted, sieved leaves, used as a peat substitute. A nonsterile medium, leaf mold may harbor pests or diseases.

GARDEN SOIL

If you are planning to use garden soil in homemade rooting media, it must first be sterilized to kill off harmful organisms. To do this, the soil must be sieved to remove stones, then heated. Use a conventional oven (30 mins at 400°F/200°C) or microwave in a pierced roasting bag on full power for ten minutes.

COMPRESSED PEAT BLOCKS

These small, biodegradable blocks of peat or coir contain a special fertilizer. The compressed blocks more than double in size when soaked in water for 10–20 minutes. A plastic mesh holds the peat together. Once soaked, they form individual planting units, and cuttings can be inserted into the hollow at the top of each block. Do not let blocks dry out, and pot or plant cuttings, complete with blocks, as soon as roots show.

SOAKED

UNSOAKED

INERT GROWING MEDIA

Different kinds of sterile, inert media can also be used for cuttings, avoiding the problem of harboring pests and diseases associated with soils and soil mixes. Damping off is also less of a problem with sterile media. The plants basically grow in water, with nutrients added directly to the water in the form of liquid fertilizer. The plants also have access to unlimited oxygen, since the plant roots are in direct contact with the air. Porous rockwool (fibers spun from mineral rock) is used in commercial trade, but other options for the gardener are florist's foam, perlite, gel, sand, pumice, or grit.

ROCKWOOL LOOSE FIBERS

ROCKWOOL LOOSE GREENMIX

ROCKWOOL UNITS, OR "CUBES"

▶FLORIST'S FOAM
Water-retentive and with a light, open texture, florist's foam can be used for soft cuttings such as fuchsias.

WATER-RETENTIVE GEL AND WATER

Water-retentive gel is commonly used in container mixes to conserve water. The dry crystals absorb water and increase in volume, forming a granular jelly. The gel can be used on its own for rooting woody cuttings, such as yew (*Taxus*): add a liquid fertilizer to the water used to hydrate the gel, insert the cuttings, and keep sealed until they root. Stem-tip cuttings of easy-to-root perennials, for example penstemons, *Solenostemon* (coleus), and *Impatiens*, may be rooted in water. Place the cuttings in a jar of water on a greenhouse bench or windowsill.

GEL
BEFORE
SOAKING

AFTER
SOAKING

▶JUST ADD WATER
Take softwood stem-tip cuttings from healthy shoots (here of coleus). Trim each cutting just below a leaf joint, then remove the lower leaves. Place netting over the jar of water to hold the cuttings in place.

Preparing Cuttings

Raising new plants from cuttings is frequently a very straightforward process, and it is certainly the most widely used technique for propagating the majority of shrubs and climbers. Gather material early in the day before the sun and rising temperatures cause plants to lose moisture through their leaves. You can either prepare the cuttings immediately or store them in plastic bags in a cool place (such as a refrigerator), out of direct sunlight, for a few hours.

How Shoots Ripen

Cuttings can be taken from different parts of a plant shoot. This shoot from a firethorn (*Pyracantha*) demonstrates the different stages of woodiness seen in a stem as a plant grows and develops. The softwood at the tip is still green, soft, and sappy, while the greenwood in the middle is less flexible. The base of the shoot is semi-ripe, becoming woody and dark.

Softwood

Semi-ripe wood

Greenwood

Trimming a Cutting

Most cuttings are taken from a plant stem; they may be severed between the leaf joints, or nodes (internodal cutting), or just below a node (nodal cutting). The growing tip may also be removed to redistribute natural growth hormones to the rest of the stem.

SELECTING THE TRIMMING POINT
Cuttings are usually trimmed just below a leaf joint, or node, where the growth hormones accumulate (see near right). Easily rooted plants can be cut between nodes (see far right).

NODAL CUTTING

INTERNODAL CUTTING

Using Fungicide and Rooting Powder

Cut large leaves in half to reduce moisture loss, and immerse very soft cuttings in fungicidal solution. Dip the base into hormone rooting compound or gel, which will encourage root formation, and insert each cutting in the medium, just deep enough for it to be able to stand upright.

FUNDAMENTAL HYGIENE
It is a good idea to wear close-fitting, sterile gloves when preparing cuttings: it helps to maintain a hygienic environment. If you have no gloves, make sure your hands are clean.

Fungicide

Hormone rooting powder

Different Types of Cutting

Cuttings are taken from stems, leaves, or roots, and there are various types, depending on the plant. In some plants, such as ivy (*Hedera*), and many in the mint family (including rosemary and salvias), preformed embryonic roots lie dormant in stems, so they root rapidly from cuttings. Quite a few woody plants may be difficult to root. It is important to choose the right type of cutting.

SOFTWOOD
CUTTING
Cotoneaster

HEEL
CUTTING
Ceanothus

LEAF-BUD
CUTTING
Clematis

ROSETTE
CUTTING
Saxifraga

LEAF
CUTTING
Sedum

HARDWOOD
CUTTING
Salix

STEM-TIP
CUTTING
Fatsia

SEMI-RIPE
CUTTING
Abelia

STEM
CUTTING
Yucca

LEAF-BUD
CUTTINGS
Mahonia

CHEVRON
LEAF CUTTING
Streptocarpus

LEAF
CUTTING
Sansevieria

BASAL STEM
CUTTING
Delphinium

ROOT
CUTTING
Ailanthus

SOFT- AND GREENWOOD CUTTINGS

SOFTWOOD CUTTINGS can be gathered from the plant from spring to early summer, before the new growth has begun to firm. This method is suitable for most deciduous shrubs and climbers and can be used for various deciduous trees, including cherries. Softwood cuttings are usually taken from fast-growing tips of new shoots and typically root very easily. Greenwood cuttings are similar to softwood but are taken when the new growth is just beginning to firm.

CHOOSING SOFTWOOD CUTTINGS

Cuttings from shrubs and climbers root most easily when the parent plant is young and producing long lengths of new growth each year. Most cuttings will be taken from wood of the current season's growth. Alternatively, use plants bought from the local garden center (which will invariably have been grown under protection) as stock plants. Increase the yield of cuttings by taking one stem-tip cutting and several stem cuttings from the same stem. The best material is usually the new growth that is neither very thin and weak, nor very vigorous; the latter is often hollow and

SOFTWOOD WALLFLOWER CUTTING

prone to rotting. Choose instead the material in between these two extremes, which normally has quite short internodal growth (the distance between two sets of leaves). This technique is also suitable for various trees, including ornamental cherries (*Prunus*), some maples (*Acer*), sweet gum (*Liquidambar*), birches (*Betula*) and elms (*Ulmus*).

GREENWOOD CUTTINGS

Greenwood cuttings can be dealt with in the same way as softwood but are taken when the new growth is just starting to firm, between late spring and midsummer. Greenwood material is easier to handle than softwood, because it doesn't wilt so readily. If you miss the softwood season, greenwood cuttings of most deciduous plants and some evergreens generally root just as well as softwoods.

SOFTWOOD CUTTING
Select sturdy, healthy new shoots in spring or early summer for softwood cuttings (here of a rose species), before they start to firm up or become woody.

GREENWOOD CUTTING
Take greenwood cuttings from vigorous current year's shoots (here of Philadelphus) that are firm and slightly woody at the base. Prepare as for softwood cuttings.

GREENWOOD CUTTINGS OF LIQUIDAMBAR
These cuttings have been trimmed at the tip above a node, and stems have been wounded. Leaves are halved to reduce moisture loss.

TAKING SOFTWOOD CUTTINGS

Softwood cuttings should usually be 1½–2in (4–5cm)long, with one to three pairs of leaves retained at the top. Gather material early in the day before temperatures begin to rise. Remove the soft tip from each cutting, because it is vulnerable to both rotting and scorch. This also ensures that, once rooted, the cutting does not immediately grow upward from the tip alone, ensuring a bushy plant from the start. Remove the lowest pair of leaves to make it easier to insert the cutting into the medium. On delicate material this should be done cleanly with a sharp knife or pruners; where there is no risk of damaging the stem, pinch off the foliage between thumb and forefinger. Dip the base in hormone rooting compound. With softwood cuttings, it is best to make a hole in the medium with a dibber or pencil.

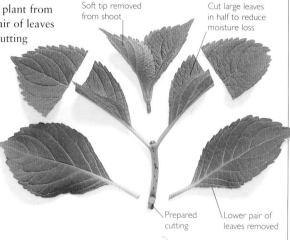

Soft tip removed from shoot

Cut large leaves in half to reduce moisture loss

Prepared cutting

Lower pair of leaves removed

1 In early spring to early summer, cut off non-flowering, vigorous shoots (here *Hydrangea macrophylla*) with 2–3 pairs of leaves. Use pruners to cut a stem just below a pair of leaves.

2 To prepare each cutting, remove the soft tip from the shoot just above a leaf, and then remove the lowest pair of leaves. The stem of the cutting should be about 1½–2in (4–5cm) in length. Cut large leaves in half to reduce moisture loss.

Propagator vent

3 Fill 5in (13cm) pots with standard rooting medium, then space the cuttings around the edge. The leaves should be just above the medium's surface and should be placed so that they are not touching.

4 Water the cuttings with a fungicidal solution, label, and place the pots in a propagator. Leave in a shaded place. Provide bottom heat of 59°F (15°C) to encourage the rooting process.

5 Once the cuttings have successfully rooted, harden them off. Gently tease apart, then pot individually into 3½in (9cm) pots. Cuttings that were pinched out will produce bushy growth.

SEMI-RIPE CUTTINGS

THIS TYPE OF CUTTING involves shoots of the current season's growth that have begun to firm up. The base of the cutting should be quite hard, while the tip of the cutting should still be actively growing and therefore still soft. This propagation method is suitable for a very wide range of woody plants, including both evergreen and deciduous species. Semi-ripe cuttings are useful for producing large numbers of plants, for example for hedging purposes.

TAKING SEMI-RIPE CUTTINGS

The best time to take semi-ripe cuttings is from mid- to late summer, or even in early autumn. In warm climates, growth may be semi-ripe in early summer. The length of the cutting is dependent on the habit of the plant, but between 2½–4in (6–10cm) is suitable for most shrubs and climbers, 4–6in (10–15cm) for broadleaved evergreens such as magnolias, laurels, and hollies. Choose a healthy stem, then remove any sideshoots to prevent moisture loss in the cutting.

1 In mid- to late summer, select a healthy shoot of the current season's growth (here from a Japanese laurel, *Aucuba*). Take cuttings early in the day and use clean, sharp pruners to sever the cutting just above a node.

2 Put the shoot in a clear plastic bag and label it if it is not to be prepared immediately. If necessary, store in a cool place out of direct sunlight for a couple of hours (at most), or place in a refrigerator for a few days.

3 Remove the sideshoots from the main stem. Trim the cutting to 4–6in (10–15cm) long, cutting just below a node. Remove the lowest pair of leaves as well as the soft tip.

4 Make a shallow wound on one side of the stem by carefully cutting away a piece of bark ½–¾in (1–2cm) long from the base of the stem. Doing this will help stimulate rooting.

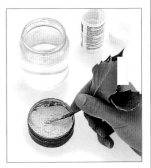

5 Dip the base of the cutting, including the entire wound, into some hormone rooting compound (here in powder form). Root with or without bottom heat, according to the plant.

Semi-ripe Cuttings of Camellia

Most camellias root from semi-ripe cuttings. They need care and a quickly draining rooting medium in cool climates, but they are easy to propagate in warmer regions. Take cuttings from midsummer to early autumn. Cuttings may be internodal or nodal (see below for variations), with ¼in (1.5cm) wounds, but nodal tip cuttings produce a flowering plant quickly, often in 3–4 years. Apply hormone rooting compound sparingly on nodal leaf-bud cuttings. Root the cuttings in humid conditions and provide bottom heat of 68°F (20°C).

| NODAL LEAF-BUD | INTERNODAL LEAF-BUD | NODAL STEM-TIP | SPLIT LEAF-BUD | THREE-NODED STEM |

Taking Heather Cuttings

There are three principal heaths and heathers: *Calluna*, *Daboecia*, and *Erica*, and propagation is always by cuttings (or layering), because seeds do not come true. Of all the heathers, cuttings from *Daboecia* and *Erica* root most readily and are least prone to disease. Take semi-ripe cuttings from healthy, vigorous, nonflowering shoots. Remove the lower leaves from *Erica* and *Daboecia* as a precaution against rot.

Use of hormone rooting compound is unnecessary, and nitrogenous fertilizer should be avoided, since heaths and heathers are sensitive to the salts. Some varieties root faster than others, so insert the cuttings individually in cells. For best results, root the cuttings in a heated propagator at 59–70°F (15–21°C). Spray or water in a general fungicide, and remember to ventilate the cuttings daily.

1 Trim each stem (here of *Calluna*) to a length of about 1½–2in (4–5cm). Hold the base of the cutting firmly, and cut straight across the stem at the appropriate point with a clean, sharp knife.

2 Stripping lower leaves from callunas is optional; lightly pinch each stem about one third from the base and quickly pull it through finger and thumb. Pinch out the tips of all cuttings.

3 Use a mixture of equal parts moist coir and peat, or equal parts fine bark and peat. Insert cuttings so that the lowest leaves just rest on the medium's surface. Do not firm in the cuttings.

TAKING CONIFER CUTTINGS

Most conifers can be raised in a variety of ways, but taking semi-ripe cuttings is the easiest for many types. Conifers are usually propagated from the current year's growth, and the basic principles are the same as for other trees and shrubs, except that conifers make new growth in two ways: main or leading shoots grow straight upward, and sideshoots grow outward. With most conifers it is very difficult for a cutting taken from a sideshoot to form a main stem (although with cypresses, there is no problem). Therefore, the best cutting material is from strong leading shoots. Cuttings taken from young (juvenile) growth usually root best.

Make sure foliage sits just above medium

1 Take clean young shoots, not adult ones with fruits. If needed, strip off the side-shoots or needles from the bottom third of each stem (here of *Chamaecyparis* 'Chilworth Silver'). The small wounds promote rooting.

2 Dip the base of each cutting in hormone rooting compound (here powder). Insert easily rooting cuttings singly in 3in (8cm) pots; make a hole, insert a cutting, firm, and water. Spray with a fungicide to prevent rot.

PIPINGS FROM PINKS AND CARNATIONS

Semi-ripe cuttings, known as "pipings," can be taken from all kinds of pinks and carnations (*Dianthus*), especially small and alpine species. Take cuttings from mid- to late summer. Once the cuttings have been removed from the plant (*see right*), dip the bases into hormone rooting compound, then insert the stems into pots of rooting medium. Place the pots in a frame or propagator and keep moist but not wet. Rooting takes 2–3 weeks at 59°F (15°C), and plants should flower the following year.

TAKING PIPINGS FROM PINKS
First, choose a healthy plant. Hold a non-flowering shoot near the base and pull out the tip. It should break easily at a node, yielding a cutting 3–4in (8–10cm) long with 3–4 pairs of leaves. Remove the lowest pair (see inset).

TAKING HEEL CUTTINGS

For plants that are difficult to root, it is a good idea to take heel cuttings, where a sideshoot is pulled from the plant so that it retains a "heel" of bark. The heel forms an area where the natural rooting hormones of the plant build up, improving chances of success in rooting the cutting. It also provides a hard end-point to the cutting, which is less prone to fungal attack. Many *Ceanothus* species are rooted in this way.

BEFORE

Trim off "tail" just below node

AFTER

1 Carefully pull away a healthy sideshoot of the current season's growth (here of a *Ceanothus*), and make sure that it comes away with a sliver, or "heel," of bark from the parent shoot. The sideshoot should be about 4in (10cm) long.

2 Trim off the "tail" of the heel with a clean, sharp knife, holding the cutting firmly. The heel contains growth hormones that will encourage rooting. Rooting is as for ordinary semi-ripe cuttings, with or without bottom heat, depending on the plant.

TAKING MALLET CUTTINGS

You can propagate *Berberis* from semi-ripe cuttings, but some species and cultivars, like *Berberis* × *lologensis*, root better from mallet cuttings. These are shoots of current growth with a piece of wood from the previous season, forming a mallet-shaped plug at the base. Apply hormone rooting compound for best results.

Semi-ripe sideshoot

Mallet

Mallet

1 Take mallet cuttings from last year's stems, in early summer for deciduous species or autumn for evergreen species. Choose short sideshoots, about 4in (10cm) long, of the current season's growth. Cut just above and below the joint on the main stem to leave a ½in (1cm) section (or "mallet") at the base of each cutting.

2 Remove the lower leaves and soft tip of each sideshoot. Slit the mallet lengthwise if its diameter is more than ¼in (5mm). Then treat the cuttings as semi-ripe cuttings. This method gives thin-stemmed cuttings a more substantial base from which to produce roots. Mallet cuttings are often used to propagate shrubs with pithy or hollow stems.

HARDWOOD CUTTINGS

MANY SHRUBS AND CLIMBERS can be propagated from hardwood cuttings, including dogwoods, willows, and honeysuckles. It is also one of the easiest and cheapest ways of raising many deciduous trees. Bush fruits, especially blackcurrants, redcurrants, and gooseberries, are also increased in this way. Long lengths of fully mature, young stems are taken after leaf fall and before new spring growth from deciduous woody plants or broadleaved evergreens.

TAKING HARDWOOD CUTTINGS

Deciduous plants are propagated from late autumn to midwinter, once the current season's growth has completely matured. Evergreen cuttings are taken at a similar time, when the leading growth bud is resting and the new growth has fully matured. Hardwood cuttings are normally much bigger than softwood or semi-ripe ones, since they are much slower to root and need extra food reserves for winter.

1 From late autumn, take well-ripened shoots of deciduous shrubs, trees, or climbers (here *Forsythia*). Remove any remaining leaves.

2 Cut off each shoot at the base of the current season's growth. Trim off the tip of each shoot if it has not ripened. Cut the shoots into 8in (20cm) sections (about the length of a pair of pruners). Make a horizontal cut just below a node at the base, then make a cut sloping away from a bud at the top.

3 Prepare a slit trench in free-draining soil: push the spade into the soil about 6in (15cm) down, then press forward. Dip the base of each cutting into rooting compound (*see inset*).

4 Insert the cuttings about 2in (5cm) apart so that about a quarter of each is visible. Rows of cuttings shuld be 12in (30cm) apart. Backfill the trench and firm the soil. Water in.

SLOW-ROOTING HARDWOOD CUTTINGS

For tree species that do not root easily, such as dawn redwoods (*Metasequoia*) or laburnums, overwinter bundles of cuttings in sand (*see right*). Each bundle should have no more than ten cuttings; otherwise, the middle ones will dry out. Sand will allow the cuttings to undergo a period of cold but will protect them against wide fluctuations in temperature. Use washed, coarse sand with a low clay content so that the surface does not form a crust. Make sure it is moist, especially after periods of frost, which can dry it out. Leave the cuttings until just before bud break in early spring, then line them out in a nursery bed.

1 Tie the cuttings (here *Metasequoia*) into bundles of up to ten cuttings. Dip into hormone rooting powder or gel.

2 Insert the bundles into a bed of sand in a sheltered place or cold frame over winter. They should root by spring.

EXTRA-LONG HARDWOOD CUTTINGS

The simplest way of propagating most fast-growing trees such as poplar and willow is to take extra-long hardwood cuttings. Take the cuttings after leaf fall and select vigorous, straight shoots up to 6ft (2m) long from the current season's growth. Remove the tip, if it is still soft, cutting back to the ripened hardwood. Trim off any sideshoots. Make planting holes with a stake or metal rod, then drop the cuttings into the holes. Firm in.

1 Select shoots (here of *Populus*) up to 6ft (2m) long from the current season's growth.

2 The cuttings are best rooted where they are to mature. Make planting holes by driving a rod into the ground to about 3ft (1m).

HARDWOOD CUTTINGS OF GRAPES

Take hardwood cuttings of grapes (*Vitis*) in late autumn. Short cuttings (known as vine eyes, containing one bud, or "eye," at the top) can also be used. Make a cut immediately above a bud and another 2in (5cm) below it. Root all grape cuttings with bottom heat.

1 Standard hardwood cuttings of grapes are taken with 3–4 buds. They root more readily than vine eyes.

STANDARD CUTTING

VINE EYE

2 When the cuttings break into bud in spring, pot them singly. Grow them on until the following spring before planting them out.

BASAL STEM CUTTINGS

MANY PERENNIALS CAN PROVIDE material for basal stem cuttings from the first flush of new growth in spring. These cuttings consist of entire young shoots severed from the crown of the parent plant, so that each retains a piece of parent tissue at the base. If taken very early in the season from summer-flowering plants such as asters, salvias, or phlox, these cuttings should make reasonably sized flowering plants by summer or autumn of the same year.

BASAL STEM CUTTINGS FROM STOCK PLANTS

Stock plants of some plants (such as chrysanthemums) can also yield basal stem cuttings if they have been overwintered under cover. The stock plants are usually then discarded, because the new plants will have much more vigor than the parent. A suitable propagating medium may be mixed from equal parts sand and peat or a peat substitute, such as coir. Some additional bottom heat will improve chances of rooting when the cuttings are taken early in the year.

1 Cut new shoots cleanly through at the junction with the woody crown tissue, ensuring the base of each cutting has a small amount of this tissue attached. These chrysanthemum cuttings are 3–4in (8–10cm) long.

2 Remove the lower leaves and trim the bases, cutting straight across below a node if visible, or so the cuttings are 2in (5cm) long. Treat the base of each chrysanthemum cutting with hormone rooting powder or gel.

Always label pots of cuttings

Lower pair of leaves removed

3 Insert the cuttings into pots of a suitable rooting medium. Water well and label clearly. Put the cuttings in a propagator, or tent them in a clear plastic bag. Since these cuttings are usually taken early in the season, bottom heat of 59°F (15°C) will speed rooting.

4 When well rooted, usually after about four weeks, separate the cuttings. Aim to keep disturbance to the roots to a minimum. Pot the cuttings singly in standard potting mix (*see inset*). Put them in a cold frame or greenhouse for growing on.

BASAL STEM CUTTINGS IN PERLITE

Basal stem cuttings of many perennials can be taken from the first new growth in spring. Even earlier cuttings can be obtained by gentle forcing of plants that have been lifted and potted in the previous autumn (as with the delphinium shown here). Forcing involves starting them into early growth in a greenhouse or cold frame. Some plants, including diascias and violas, can be induced to form material suitable for basal stem cuttings later in the season: cut back flowered stems to the crown and top-dress it with gritty soil mix. Some perennials, notably lupines and delphiniums, have hollow stems that tend to rot in soil mix. Taking basal stem cuttings seals the stem against rot, since the base of the cutting has a piece of crown attached. For hollow-stemmed cuttings, a light, open medium such as perlite or vermiculite helps prevent rot; regularly spray or drench the cuttings with fungicide. Bottom heat of 59°F (15°C) improves rooting.

Stubs are removed from lower stem

1 Select new shoots that are about 3–4in (8–10cm) long, in spring. Cut off at the base, keeping a piece of the parent's woody crown. Trim off all except the top 2–3 leaves. With a clean sharp knife, remove any stubs.

2 Remove any damaged tissue. Fill a 6in (15cm) pot with moist perlite to within 1in (2.5cm) of the rim. Stand the pot in a saucer of water. Gently push in about 8 cuttings so that they are half-buried.

3 Label the pot, then put both pot and saucer in a warm place out of direct sunlight. Keep the perlite constantly moist. The cuttings should root in 4–8 weeks and are ready for potting when the new roots are about ½in (1cm) long. Ease them out gently.

4 Shake off any loose perlite. Pot the rooted cuttings singly into 3in (8cm) pots of soilless potting mix, at the same depth as before. Firm gently, label, and water. Grow on the cuttings for 6–8 weeks until they are established before planting them out.

LEAF-BUD CUTTINGS

OFTEN TAKEN FROM SHRUBS AND CLIMBERS, leaf-bud cuttings make economical use of softwood and semi-ripe material from the parent plant, producing several cuttings from one vigorous shoot. A leaf-bud cutting requires only a short piece of stem to provide food reserves, since it also manufactures some food through its leaves. Take cuttings in spring or summer.

TAKING LEAF-BUD CUTTINGS

Leaf-bud cuttings can be internodal (cut between leaf joints), which usually works well with clematis and honeysuckle, or nodal (cut below a leaf joint), which is

CAMELLIA CUTTING

more suitable for plants with hollow stems or ones that are susceptible to rot, such as camellias. Cut off a strong shoot and sever it between the nodes to create a number of internodal cuttings, each with one or two leaves. Take care to retain the growth buds in the leaf joint at the tip; they are all too easily nipped out in error. With some species the buds are quite long; in this case the cutting should be cut back to just slightly above the top pair of leaves. You may need to wound very woody stems by cutting away bark from the stem base, but this is not generally necessary.

LEAF-BUD CUTTINGS OF CLEMATIS

Leaf-bud cuttings of softwood are taken from spring to midsummer and of semi-ripe wood from mid- to late summer. They all root well, but semi-ripe cuttings need less humidity. For large-leaved cuttings such as *Clematis montana* cultivars and *C. armandii*, reduce the cutting to a single leaf to avoid overcrowding and gray mold. Take internodal leaf-bud cuttings about 2in (5cm) long from the current season's growth. Look for well-formed buds; weak buds may not produce new shoots.

STRONG BUDS

WEAK BUDS

PREPARED CUTTING

ROOTING TIMES

- The time taken for a cutting to root depends upon the plant, the type of cutting, age of the stem, how it was prepared, and the rooting environment.
- Leafy cuttings root in about three weeks; woody cuttings take up to five months. Leaf-bud cuttings generally take about eight weeks to root, depending on the woodiness of the stem.

PLANTS FOR LEAF-BUD CUTTINGS

Camellia japonica and *C. × williamsii* cultivars.
Clematis All species and cultivars.
Dracaena fragrans and cultivars, *D. marginata* 'Tricolor'. Variegated cultivars must be grown from cuttings to retain variegation.
Ficus elastica (rubber plant) and cultivars.
Hedera canariensis, H. colchica and *H. helix* cultivars (ivy).

Lonicera japonica, L. periclymenum, L. sempervirens and other climbing species (honeysuckle).
Mahonia aquifolium, M. japonica, M. × media and other species and cultivars.
Passiflora caerulea and other species (passionflower).
Philodendron scandens and other species.
Rubus cockburnianus and other species (brambles).

LEAF-BUD CUTTINGS FROM SHRUBS AND CLIMBERS

Leaf-bud cuttings are made up of a single leaf or a pair of leaves containing a growth bud and a short piece of stem. If appropriate for the plant (see *Taking Leaf-bud Cuttings* on facing page), divide a section of stem into nodal cuttings by cutting each one just below a leaf joint. If the plant has large leaves, such as *Lonicera* (honeysuckle), it is a good idea to cut them in half to reduce moisture loss. Apply hormone rooting compound to the base of each cutting, shaking off the excess if using powder. Insert the cuttings around the edge of a pot filled with standard rooting medium. After watering in with fungicide solution and labeling, keep the cuttings humid by placing them in a propagator or under a plastic film tent. Some less hardy plants may need bottom heat to aid rooting. Cuttings take around eight weeks to root. Pot the young plants into single containers using potting mix and grow them on in protected conditions until established, then harden off and plant out.

1 Select a healthy shoot of the current season's growth (here of ivy, *Hedera*). Cut the stem just above every node to create inter-nodal cuttings with 1–2 leaves. Prepare nodal cuttings by trimming below a leaf at the base and above a leaf at the top.

2 Dip each prepared cutting (*see inset*) in some hormone rooting compound. Fill a pot with standard rooting medium, then make holes for the cuttings. Insert each cutting into the medium so that the leaves are held just above the surface and do not touch.

Leaf-bud cuttings in pots

Vent

3 Firm and water in the cuttings and label the pots. Place the pots in a propagator and keep the environment more humid by misting if needed. Bottom heat is generally not required for ivies. The cuttings should take about 8 weeks to root.

4 Pot the rooted cuttings individually in standard soilless potting mix, into pots about ½in (1cm) larger than the root ball of each cutting (*see inset*). Water in each cutting thoroughly and label. Grow on until the plants are well established.

LEAF CUTTINGS

SOME PLANTS CAN REGENERATE roots and shoots from part or whole leaves (although variegated plants cannot be used for this purpose). There are two types of leaf cutting: with the first, the whole leaf is used, and with the second, new plants form on the surface or cut edge of a sectioned leaf, as in *Streptocarpus* and *Sansevieria*. Leaf cuttings are usually taken early in the growing season.

SUCCULENT LEAF CUTTINGS

Some types of succulent, for example many species of *Crassula*, *Kalanchoe*, and *Echeveria*, may be propagated from leaf cuttings. Take the cuttings, selecting firm fleshy leaves, and pot them as shown. Place in a bright position (shielded from direct sun), and keep slightly damp. The leaves should produce roots after two to four weeks. After another month, tiny new plantlets will develop.

1 Fill a pot with gritty soil topped with coarse sand. Push the base of each leaf (here *Pachyphytum oviferum*) deep enough into the sand for the leaf to stand up.

2 Label and place in a bright, warm, airy position. Keep slightly moist. After 1–6 months, the leaves should have rooted and produced new plantlets.

WHOLE-LEAF CUTTINGS

This method involves a whole leaf and its stalk, and sometimes a dormant bud at the base of the stalk where it joined the stem.

On African violets (*Saintpaulia*) the bud is not needed, because a new one will form. The cuttings need a freely draining medium.

Improvised cloche

1 Cut healthy, mature leaves (here of African violet) from the parent plant, close to the base of the leaf stalk. Insert in pots of equal parts peat and coarse sand.

2 Water the cuttings. Allow to drain. Cover to prevent moisture loss: here, clear plastic bottles are cut down to make cloches. Provide bottom heat and shade from sunlight.

3 Remove the covers after several plantlets have formed around each leaf base. Allow the new plants to grow on until they are large enough to be potted singly.

PART-LEAF CUTTINGS

With this method, new plants form from the wounded veins of a sectioned leaf. *Streptocarpus* is shown here; sansevierias can be propagated from transverse sections (*see p.29*). Plantlets appear along the veins; when they are large enough, pot up.

1 Select a healthy, full-grown leaf and cut it into sections, so that the veins in the leaf are wounded. Here a *Streptocarpus* leaf is cut in half and the midrib discarded. Prepare a seed tray of free-draining rooting medium.

2 Make shallow trenches in the medium, then insert the leaf cuttings in them, cut side down. Firm gently around the base of the cuttings. Put the tray in a propagator or seal in a plastic bag to prevent moisture loss.

LEAF CUTTINGS FROM BEGONIAS

Leaf cuttings root readily from *Begonia rex*, *B. masoniana*, and similar types. Take leaf cuttings in spring or summer; plantlets should form in about six weeks to two months. Two different techniques are illustrated here.

1 Select a fully grown, healthy leaf (here of *Begonia rex*). Using a sharp knife, cut off the leaf stalk and then cut straight across each of the main veins on the underside of the leaf. Each cut is ½in (1cm) long.

2 Pin the leaf, cut side down, onto the surface of a tray of standard rooting medium or vermiculite. Pin down the veins to keep them in contact with the medium. Label the tray. Keep humid at 70°F (21°C) until plantlets develop, in around two months.

3 Alternatively, cut squares, about 1in (2.5cm) across, from a large, healthy leaf. Each square must have a main vein running through it. Secure them with pins, veins downward, in a tray of rooting medium, then treat as in Step 2.

ROOT AND RHIZOME CUTTINGS

A LIMITED RANGE OF PLANTS – ones that naturally produce shoots, or suckers from the roots, such as *Rhus typhina* – can be propagated from root cuttings. The roots are usually thick and fleshy, since they store food for producing shoots. Some plants, such as pulsatillas, grow well from root cuttings, but there will be a check in growth from the root disturbance. Cuttings can also be taken from mature rhizomes (swollen underground stems).

TAKING ROOT CUTTINGS OF ACANTHUS

Acanthus species increase naturally from roots left in the soil, and they are easy to propagate from root cuttings. Lengths of healthy root can be taken in the dormant season, of pencil or medium thickness for the plant. Cuttings flower in two years.

1 Lift the plant in autumn or winter when it is dormant, then wash the roots. Choose strong roots of medium thickness for the plant, then sever them, cutting as close to the crown as possible. Remove no more than one-third of the available root material.

2 Cut each root into sections that are 2–4in (5–10cm) long; making the thinner cuttings the longest. To make sure that you insert the cuttings the right way up in the medium, cut the base of each cutting at an angle, and cut the top of each straight across (*see inset*).

3 Prepare pots of moist rooting medium. Treat the cuttings with a fungicide. Use a dibber to make holes as deep as the cuttings, then insert them vertically. The top of each should be level with the medium surface. Top-dress with a layer of coarse sand.

4 When new top growth appears, usually by the following spring, gently tease out the cuttings and check for root growth. When ready, pot the cuttings individually in 3in (8cm) pots filled with standard potting mix. Water well, then label the pots.

CUTTINGS OF CULINARY HERBS

Herbs with creeping roots (such as horseradish) or rhizomes (such as mint) can be propagated by root or rhizome cuttings. Take the cuttings in spring or autumn. Lift the parent plant, then remove some healthy roots or rhizomes. With most herbs, including mint, they should be of average thickness. Horseradish roots root readily whichever way up they are, so they can be sliced into small sections. Keep the cuttings in a bright place, but out of direct sunlight. Do not water until new roots or top-growth appear (2–3 weeks).

Roots are sliced into ½in (1cm) sections

1 In spring, lift a healthy horseradish plant, taking care not to damage the roots. Cut off 1–2 lengths of root, 6–12in (15–30cm) long. Prepare a container with rooting medium, then firm.

2 Slice the roots into ½in (1cm) sections. Insert each cutting 1–2½in (2.5–6cm) deep in the prepared cell tray. When the cuttings have good root systems, transplant to their final positions.

TAKING RHIZOME CUTTINGS OF BERGENIA

Rhizomes are usually swollen underground stems, either thick, as in bearded irises; thin and fast-growing, as with wild rye (*Elymus*); or in a crown, as in asparagus. As a rhizome grows, it often develops segments, each with buds that break into growth when conditions are favorable. These can be cut apart for propagation.

Bergenias form woody, creeping rhizomes, often on the soil surface, with leaves only at their tips. Detach these with some roots then transplant them, if just a few plants are desired. To produce large numbers of new plants, take rhizome cuttings. Cut the older part of the rhizomes, which are devoid of leaves, into sections.

1 Cut older pieces of leafless rhizome into 1½–2 in (4–5cm) sections, each with several dormant buds, in autumn. Trim any long roots. Half-bury the sections, buds uppermost, about 2in (5cm) apart in trays in moist perlite or soil mix. Water and label.

2 Keep the cuttings at a humid 70°F (21°C) in a heated propagator, shaded to prevent dehydration. After 10–12 weeks, plantlets (here of *Bergenia cordifolia*) should have rooted. Pot singly or line out in a nursery bed in spring. Flowering occurs in 1–2 years.

SPECIALIZED CUTTINGS

THESE VARIATIONS ARE USED to propagate specialist's plants. Rosette cuttings are taken from some, including cushion-forming alpines and various succulents. Certain shrubs, trees, and perennials, including *Yucca*, *Cordyline*, (cabbage palm) and *Dieffenbachia* (dumb cane), are increased from leafless stem sections. Stem cuttings without leaves can be used to propagate some columnar and epiphytic or forest cacti.

ROSETTE CUTTINGS IN GROUND PUMICE

Cuttings can be taken from rosette-forming alpines in late spring and in summer. Handle parent plants with care, for they are easily damaged. The short-stemmed cuttings also need careful handling. Use ground pumice, if possible, for difficult alpines. Derived from Icelandic volcanic rock, it is totally sterile and sufficiently water-retentive for alpines. Rooting of rosette cuttings is slow and unreliable, however.

1 Select a healthy rosette from the edge of the plant (here *Dionysia aretioides*). Cut the stem ¼–½in (5–10mm) below the shoot tip. Trim lower leaves, then dip base into hormone rooting compound.

2 Fill a 2in (5cm) clay pot with ground pumice to within ½in (1cm) of the rim. Water from below and allow to drain. Insert the cuttings ½in (1cm) apart. Firm around them, then label the pot.

LEAFLESS STEM SECTIONS

Various plants, such as stem-producing yuccas, cordylines, and dieffenbachias, can be increased from leafless stem sections. Cuttings of all are usually inserted vertically into the rooting medium, but yucca cuttings can be laid flat to induce young shoots for use as softwood cuttings. The cut-back stems of parent plants will reshoot.

1 Remove a 12–36in (30–90cm) section from a mature stem (here *Yucca elephantipes*), cutting between the leaf nodes. Strip all the foliage. Cut the stem into 4in (10cm) cuttings.

2 Trim alternately above and below a node. Press the cuttings flat into moist soilless rooting medium so they are half buried, or insert vertically into 3½in (9cm) pots.

Succulent Rosette Cuttings

Some rosette-forming succulents consist of clumps of rosettes. These can be severed at the base, then rooted as shown here. Once potted, keep the cuttings in a bright, airy position.

1 Using a sharp clean knife, cut 2–3in (5–8cm) from the top of a young rosette of leaves (here of *Echeveria* 'Frosty'). Trim off the bottom leaves (*see inset*), then allow to callus for a few days.

2 Gently push the stem through the sand top-dressing into the medium so the leaves sit just above the surface. Use a standard 3in (8cm) pot or a deep seed tray.

Flat Stem Cuttings from Cacti

Some epiphytic, or forest, cacti such as epiphyllums and Christmas cacti (*Schlumbergera*) will root from sections of their flat, leaflike stems. These cacti generally prefer a more humid environment than desert types and prefer partial shade. Take a whole mature stem from the parent plant at the base in late spring or early summer, after flowering.

Tip of stem is top of cutting

1 Cut a flattened stem (here of an *Epiphyllum*) into 9in (23cm) sections. Allow to callus for a few days. Fill a pot with cactus soil mix.

2 Fill the pot to just below the rim. Cover the mix with a shallow layer of coarse sand, then push the cutting into the medium below.

Stem Cuttings of Columnar Cacti

Cuttings up to 6ft (2m) long can be taken from columnar cacti such as the monstrose form of *Cereus hildmannianus*, shown here. The larger the wound on the cutting, the longer it will take to callus. Cuttings should root in 1–12 months.

1 Wear thick gloves and use a folded cloth to steady the plant. Use a large knife to remove a 3in–3ft (8cm–1m) length.

2 Leave the cutting in a warm, dry place to callus (2–3 weeks in summer). Fill the bottom third of a pot with cactus soil, then add a layer of fine gravel. Stand the cutting on this, then fill with gravel to the top. Keep slightly moist.

CARING FOR CUTTINGS

PROPAGATING UNDER COVER

ONCE ANY PLANT MATERIAL has been correctly prepared for propagation and inserted into a suitable growing medium, it is important to provide conditions that will enable the material to survive and establish. The degree of care needed depends on the species of plant and the mode of propagation. Hardwood cuttings, for example, require minimal care, but leafy cuttings taken in summer from a difficult plant will need a closely regulated environment.

PROVIDING THE RIGHT SUPPORT

Propagation involving regenerative processes, such as the formation of new roots or shoots, immediately demands some form of environmental support until the new plants become independent. In cooler climates, favorable conditions can often only be achieved under cover – for instance, in the home, conservatory, or greenhouse –

to extend the growing season or increase tender plants. For outdoor propagation, cold frames, cloches, or nursery beds offer a degree of shelter. In warmer regions, windbreaks, shading structures, and irrigation systems may be required.

Propagating plants away from their natural or adapted habitat makes them vulnerable to attacks from pests and diseases, so the propagation area should be kept as clean as possible.

In general, cuttings need water, warmth, air, light, and sometimes nutrients to root. The humidity of the air is a critical issue for many unrooted leafy cuttings, for example. In spring and summer they may need 98–100 percent humidity to prevent wilting. Plants are temperature-dependent and grow best when warm. Ventilation helps prevent fungal infection such as botrytis, but it must also be regulated to avoid excessive loss of humidity.

TENTING

The easiest way to keep humid air around cuttings is to create a tent with a clear plastic bag. Hold the bag clear of the plant material with a wire hoop or stakes.

◀ CONTROLLED ENVIRONMENT *A necessity for many cuttings, easily achieved in a greenhouse.*

WINDOWSILL PROPAGATION

The simplest propagation environment can be created by keeping individual containers on a bright windowsill or in a glassed-in porch or conservatory. The location provides warmth and light; humidity is maintained by covering the container. For a pot of cuttings, use a plastic bag or a beverage bottle. Whichever type of cover is used, it must be kept clear of the cuttings.

Lid redirects moist air back to the plants and maintains humidity

◄ HOME-GROWN
It need not be difficult to root cuttings at home. A bright windowsill is suitable for cuttings.

► HEATED HOME
Portable propagators can be used indoors. Some are fitted with electric heating elements to provide bottom heat.

▲ RETAINING A HUMID ATMOSPHERE
Propagated material such as leafy cuttings must often be kept in a contained space to keep the air humid. Moisture from the cuttings rises to the top of the propagator. The cover stops moisture from evaporating, and the vent allows excess humidity to be controlled.

Cells make the most of the space

CHOOSING A GREENHOUSE

A greenhouse is a valuable asset in cooler climates, allowing varying degrees of environmental regulation. There are many different styles available. Some models are designed for maximum light penetration, heat conservation, or ventilation, while others make the best use of restricted space.

There are four categories: cold (unheated), cool, temperate, and warm; the choice depends on the plants you want to grow.

A lean-to or mini-greenhouse benefits from the warmth and insulation of the house wall, but it may suffer more from extreme temperature changes.

PLASTIC TUNNEL
This low-cost greenhouse is covered with heavy-duty film plastic, which will eventually become opaque.

MINI-GREENHOUSE
This is very useful where space is limited. Choose a position carefully for maximum heat and light.

TRADITIONAL GREENHOUSE
This allows the most complete and controlled propagation environment. Different areas can be created for various uses.

THE PROPAGATOR'S GREENHOUSE

A greenhouse provides the gardener with the chance to create various separate environments for propagating and growing plants. This greenhouse is equipped with all the elements necessary to propagate a wide range of plants. Insulation or heating may be needed in winter.

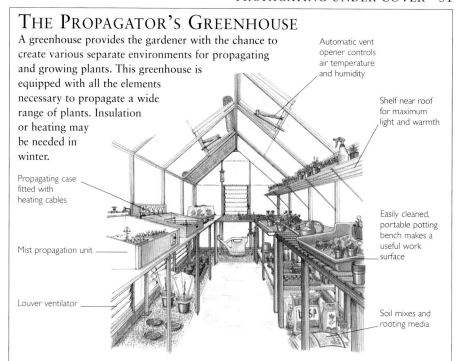

Automatic vent opener controls air temperature and humidity

Shelf near roof for maximum light and warmth

Propagating case fitted with heating cables

Easily cleaned, portable potting bench makes a useful work surface

Mist propagation unit

Louver ventilator

Soil mixes and rooting media

PROVIDING AN EXTRA BOOST FOR CUTTINGS

The temperature of the growing environment will affect plant growth. A heated propagator provides thermostatically controlled bottom heat, ensuring that the growing medium is warmer than the air above. Soil-warming cables, sold in varying lengths and wattages, can be used. More sophisticated systems such as mist and fog propagators (*see p.13*) offer the additional bonus of regulated air humidity.

Sand bed

Cable also heats air

Air thermostat

Soil thermostat

Control box

Stop valve

Misting head

Soil-warming cable

Drainage hole

Soil thermostat

USING SOIL-WARMING CABLES
Lay the cable in a series of "S" bends in a bed of moist sand at a depth of 2–3 in (5–8cm), making sure the loops do not touch.

INSIDE A MIST PROPAGATOR
As well as supplying bottom heat through an electrically heated bed of sand or medium, a mist of fine water droplets is sprayed.

CLOCHES AND COLD FRAMES

I N THE OPEN GARDEN IN COOLER CLIMATES, cloches and cold frames may be used to warm the soil and air, increase local humidity, and give shelter from drying winds and some protection from pests. They can provide a suitable rooting environment for a wide range of easily rooted cuttings. Cold frames are more permanent structures than cloches. They may also be used for overwintering rooted cuttings and for the hardening off of new plants.

DIFFERENT TYPES OF CLOCHE

Cloches provide a suitable rooting environment for a variety of easily rooted cuttings. A wide range of designs and materials is available. The best are glass or plastic; plastic allows less light penetration and retains less heat. Plastic film and rigid polypropylene last five years or more; rigid, twin-walled polycarbonate lasts for at least ten years. Well-fitting end pieces are essential to stop the cloche from becoming a wind tunnel. Rigid cloches are more

costly but more easily moved, making watering and transplanting easier. Some are self-watering, with permeable coverings that allow rainwater to trickle through.

▶ SELF-WATERING CLOCHE
This type of cloche is designed to allow rain-water, or water from a garden sprinkler, to trickle through to the plants or cuttings below.

PLASTIC FILM TUNNEL
Sturdy wire hoops are covered by plastic film, which allows easy accessibility. Tying the plastic prevents the interior from becoming a wind tunnel.

RIGID PLASTIC TUNNEL
This type of plastic cloche can be any length and is held in position by a metal or plastic frame. The rigid plastic should last 5 years or more.

TENT CLOCHE
Simply constructed from two sheets of glass to form a tent shape, this kind of cloche can be used singly or in a row to cover low plants and cuttings.

The Advantages of a Cold Frame

Cold frames provide propagation material and new plants with higher soil and air temperatures, reduced temperature fluctuation if shaded and ventilated, shelter from winds, and adequate light levels. Cold frames also suit certain plant material, such as gray-foliaged Mediterranean plants or hardwood cuttings, that do not like the humidity of a closed case or propagator. Cuttings can be inserted directly to root in a nursery bed in the frame. A good number of pots or trays can be accommodated in a cold frame, and soil-warming cables (*see p.51*) may also be used in the bed.

◀ MOVABLE COLD FRAME
This portable cold frame may be moved around to take advantage of seasonal light.

▲ FIXED COLD FRAME
This brick frame (with glass removed for sunny days) holds heat and excludes drafts.

Using a Cold Frame

Cold frames with metal frameworks let in the most light and can be moved around the garden to follow the best light at different times of year, but they do not retain heat or exclude drafts as well as wood and brick frames. Permanent frames must be sited in a sheltered position and where maximum light is received all year.

Cold frames overheat in sun unless they are ventilated and shaded. If the temperature falls below freezing, insulate the frame to avoid cold damage.

Warmed air escapes

Cool air enters and absorbs heat

AIR CIRCULATION
Cold air expands and rises as it heats up on a warm day. Open the lights of the frame to allow some warm air to escape; the inside temperature should remain reasonably cool.

Line the base with broken clay pots for drainage

Add 6in (15cm) of rooting medium

FILLING A PERMANENT COLD FRAME
A fixed frame can provide a nursery bed for cuttings. Cover the base with a thick layer of drainage material, such as broken clay pots or coarse gravel. Fill with rooting medium.

CARE OF CUTTINGS UNDER COVER

THE CHOICE OF GROWING MEDIUM should provide the propagated material with an appropriate amount of oxygen and nutrients, but correct watering and temperature control of the medium is also needed for the various growth processes to occur (such as root initiation). Long summer days help with propagation, but intense light will overheat the air, in turn causing excessive transpiration and stress to cuttings. Shading to create indirect light aids rooting.

IMPORTANCE OF WARMTH AND HUMIDITY

The humidity of the air affects the rate at which plants transpire, or allow water to evaporate from leaf pores. The more humid the air, the less the plants transpire (*see p.50*). This is a critical issue for unrooted leafy cuttings, which in spring and summer need a very humid atmosphere to prevent wilting. Wilted cuttings have a reduced ability to regenerate, form callus tissue, or develop roots. Cuttings absorb moisture through their severed bases more quickly than through leaves, but once callus tissue forms, water can be taken in only by the leaves. Excessive transpiration can cause stress in cuttings, resulting in leaf drop, but it can be controlled by shading (*see below*).

GROWN
WITHOUT
HEAT

BENEFITS OF HEAT
If the temperature of the rooting medium is warmer than the air, cuttings usually root more quickly and strongly (see p.51).

GROWN
WITH HEAT

VENTILATION AND SHADING

Shading should protect plant material from being scorched by direct sun while still allowing sufficient light to pass through it for good growth. Direct sunlight heats the air, causing stress in cuttings due to excessive transpiration. Some shading materials used on greenhouses include shading washes, while shading netting can be used on smaller structures. Excess heat can also be controlled by ventilating the propagating environment.

AUTOMATIC VENTING
Adequate ventilation is essential to control air temperature and humidity in a greenhouse. An automatic vent opener controls both of these elements by opening automatically when the temperature rises above a predetermined level.

▲ SHADING WASH
In warm weather, shading will help control air temperature in a greenhouse. Washes make very effective shading, because they significantly reduce the heat from the sun while allowing through enough light for good growth. Apply the wash externally.

WATERING AND AFTERCARE

It is important to provide a regular and adequate supply of water for cuttings, especially in hot or windy weather, and particular attention should be paid to plants growing in smaller containers, which can dry out quickly. Adequate water is crucial for good plant growth; however, an excess of water (waterlogging) can be just as damaging as lack of water, since it will deprive the roots of oxygen and promote rot. Possibly more cuttings are lost in this way than for any other reason.

FINE BRASS
NOZZLE

WATERING IN CUTTINGS
Use a fine nozzle turned upward to water cuttings (here of rosemary). It creates a fine, light spray and avoids disturbing the medium.

AVOIDING PLANT PROBLEMS

Propagated plants live in an artificial environment that leaves them vulnerable to attack from harmful pests and diseases. The use of bottom heat, frequent watering, and high humidity that are so often essential in propagation also encourage the proliferation of debilitating fungal diseases, for example. These are often introduced through poor hygiene in the preparation of plant material or through contaminated media. Pests and diseases can also be transmitted from the parent plant; this can be a particular problem with pests that are not easily detectable, such as nematodes.

Regularly check new plants, and control any problems as soon as they arise. Cuttings that show signs of rot, viruses, or cold damage should be discarded as soon as the problem is noted. It is best to try to prevent plant problems from occurring in the first place. Observe good hygiene, use sharp, clean instruments for cutting, and use sterile growing media. Greenhouses should be scrubbed annually with a disinfectant solution ; this will help control fungus gnats, whiteflies, spider mites, mildew, and the various fungi that cause blackleg (and damping off of seedlings).

BLACKLEG
Before or as roots form, the base of a cutting darkens and atrophies; the upper parts discolor and die. It is caused by soil- or water-borne fungi.

GREENHOUSE WHITEFLY
These sap-feeding insects cause stunted growth and distorted leaves. Use insecticidal soaps and/or biological control.

GRAY MOLD
Gray mold (Botrytis cinerea) thrives in damp conditions, and spores may persist from year to year. Increase air circulation around plants.

THE ROOTED CUTTINGS

ONCE THE CUTTINGS HAVE ROOTED, they need special care to get them acclimatized to the growing environment. They must be slowly weaned from the cossetted conditions in which they have been raised, they will need potting, and plants intended for outdoors must be hardened off in a cold frame.

WEANING PROPAGATED PLANTS

Once plants have functioning root and shoot systems that are adequate for independent survival, the process of weaning them from the propagation environment into a growing environment should take place. Cuttings that have been rooted in closed propagating cases, under plastic film on a heated bench, or in mist or fog propagation units need particular care. It takes two to three weeks for plants to fully acclimatize. First, any bottom heat is turned off. The humidity level is then gradually reduced, plastic film and propagator covers are removed for a longer period each day until eventually they are not replaced at night, and the duration and frequency of mist or fog bursts are reduced; then the units are switched off at night. Once weaned, place the new plants in temperatures appropriate to the species.

Growing on heaths and heathers, as shown here, is a good example of how to treat many other hardy shrubs once the cuttings have rooted under cover.

1 Heath and heather cuttings should root after about 8–12 weeks. To keep them growing vigorously, start fertilizing weekly. Pinch out the growing tips to encourage bushy new growth. Provide shade as necessary, since direct sun causes stress in young plants and scorches foliage. Ventilate plants daily.

Bushy young plants ready for planting

2 The well-rooted cuttings are potted individually into 3–3½in (8–9cm) pots, using acidic soil mix for lime-hating heathers. Grow on outdoors after hardening off in a cold frame. The hardening-off process should take place over a period of two to three weeks.

3 When large enough, plant out in flowering positions. A good time for planting heathers and other young shrubs is autumn, while the soil is still relatively warm. This encourages plants to rapidly make new roots and become established before cold weather sets in. The alternative is spring planting.

POTTING TENDER PLANTS

When cuttings are well rooted, carefully transfer each one singly into a pot filled with potting mix. The pot should not be too large. Colorful-leaved coleus (*Solenostemon*), shown here, are popular and not difficult from cuttings.

Four-week old cuttings

1 The cuttings have been placed in rockwool cubes (*see inset*) in a propagator to keep humid, and in bright light at a minimum temperature of 64–70°F (18–21°C). Roots develop after about two weeks.

2 Pot the rooted cuttings singly into 3½in (9cm) pots of soilless potting mix. Do not tease out the roots from rockwool cubes. Grow the young plants in a warm, bright place.

HARDENING OFF AND PINCHING OUT

Before planting out, young plants raised under cover must be hardened off by acclimatizing them to the temperatures outdoors. This may take two to three weeks and must not be rushed, because the plant's leaves must undergo changes to reduce water loss. Transferring the young plants to a cold frame is ideal – ventilate gradually until the covers are fully open at night as well as by day. A cloche is an alternative but does not offer as much cold protection. Encourage bushy growth by pinching out growing tips.

▶ PINCHING OUT
Pinching out the growing tip encourages sideshoots and a bushier plant.

OPENING HINGED LIGHTS (COVERS)
A cold frame is ideal for hardening off. Hinged lights can be propped open to stop plants from overheating but may admit wind.

OPENING SLIDING LIGHTS
Sliding lights can be removed entirely if desired, but this would leave plants unprotected in the event of heavy rain.

CUTTINGS IN THE OPEN

SOME CUTTINGS, PARTICULARLY many hardwood cuttings of woody plants, are rooted outdoors directly in the soil. Very often, after hardening off, young hardy plants are planted out in a nursery bed to grow on for a year or two. For both of these, you will need to thoroughly prepare some beds in a sheltered position, possibly provide protection from the elements, prevent them from drying out, and watch out for a number of pests and diseases.

SIMPLE DIGGING

Soil beds intended for hardwood cuttings or young plants are prepared by single digging (to one depth of the spade blade), which is best done several months before the beds are needed. During the digging, add plenty of bulky organic matter, such as old compost, to each trench to help the soil retain moisture. If the drainage is poor, also add coarse to each trench, and mix some into the topsoil.

1 Simple digging just involves turning over spadefuls of soil. Drive the spade down to its full depth, keeping the blade upright. Press down firmly with the ball of your foot.

2 Pull back on the handle and lever soil on to the blade. Bend your knees and elbows to lift the spade; do not try to lift too much at once, especially where the soil is heavy.

PROTECTING YOUNG PLANTS

Outdoor nursery beds do not have the controlled environment found under cover and so may need some form of protection. Drying winds can stress plant material by increasing moisture loss: construct windbreaks on the side of the prevailing winds, or use covers. In warm climates or dry seasons, beds may also need irrigation: seep hoses are useful and can be laid alongside new plants.

WIND PROTECTION
To protect cuttings and young plants from cold, drying winds, erect a screen of windbreak netting on the windward side. This filters and slows down the wind.

SHADING
Supporting plastic netting over young plants prevents new growth from being scorched by the sun, particularly during hot summers or in warm climates.

DEALING WITH PROBLEMS

Most plant problem symptoms are easy to see, from mold to visible insects. Check plants frequently to spot any problems as soon as they arise. Do not allow young plants or cuttings to dry out, and make sure the soil has adequate nutrients for healthy growth. Observe good hygiene, and try to use organic methods of control before resorting to chemicals.

CUTWORMS
These gnaw on roots and stem bases and feed on the soil surface at night. Find all of the cutworms and destroy.

POWDERY MILDEW
White, powdery fungal growth appears on leaves. Remove infected leaves immediately, and avoid overhead watering.

COLD DAMAGE
The upper parts of leaves turn brown or black. Nip off affected leaves, or discard badly damaged plants.

SLUGS
These feed on soft plant material, mainly at night or after rain. Hand-pick or use slug pellets, barriers, or traps.

BLACK VINE WEEVIL LARVAE
These grubs feed on roots. Plants grow slowly, wilt, and die. Use biological control or insecticides.

IRREGULAR WATERING
Adequate water is crucial for good plant growth, and cuttings must be regularly watered to avoid wilting.

APHIDS
These sap-feeding insects cause stunted growth and distorted leaves. Control with insecticidal soap.

IRON AND MANGANESE DEFICIENCY
Leaf discoloration means plants may need acidic soil. Apply chelated iron.

VIRUSES
Many viruses are transmitted from infected plants by sap-feeding insects. Destroy all affected plants promptly.

PLANTS TO GROW FROM CUTTINGS

A wide range of plants can be grown from cuttings – trees, shrubs, climbers, perennials (including alpines), and cacti and succulents. You can take cuttings from your own plants and perhaps exchange them with gardening friends.

◉ *Prefers full sun* ◲ *Prefers partial shade* ▣ *Tolerates full shade* ◊ *Prefers well-drained soil* ◓ *Prefers moist soil* ◆ *Prefers wet soil* Z *Hardiness zone ranges are given as Zx–x. Hardiness of individual species or selections is usually much less broad than the range given for the entire genus.*

GARDEN TREES

S MALL ORNAMENTAL TREES help form the permanent structure of a garden. They are expensive to buy, but many are surprisingly easy to propagate from cuttings, so you could have a small group of young trees or even grow some as shrubs by coppicing them regularly.

Acer
(Maple)
Moderately easy to propagate from softwood cuttings in early summer. Take cuttings from fast-growing tips of new shoots, and make sure they do not wilt. Remove growing tip if cutting is longer than 4in (10cm). Root in a closed propagating case with bottom heat of 64–75°F (18–24°C).
◉–◲◊ Z3–9

Ailanthus altissima
(Tree of heaven)
Easy to propagate from root cuttings in early winter. Choose roots about ½in (1cm) in diameter, but do not wash them. Root in a cool place, such as a slightly heated greenhouse. When rooted, in 3–4 months, line out in nursery bed or pot up. This tree can be coppiced.
◉–◲◊ Z4–8

Betula
(Birch)
Moderately easy from softwood cuttings taken from midspring to early summer. Root in a propagator with bottom heat of 64–75°F (18–24°C). Fertilize regularly once they have rooted to encourage maximum growth in first season; otherwise, they may fail to start into growth in the following spring.
◉–◲◓ Z2–8

ACER PALMATUM 'ÔSAKAZUKI'

◀ A CLASSIC SHRUB BORDER *A scene like this could be created from cuttings.*

CORDYLINE AUSTRALIS
'VARIEGATA'

Cordyline
(Cabbage palm)
Easily propagated from leaf-less stem sections at any time. Prepare from strong side shoots, each section with one or two nodes. Insert in shallow pans or half pots. Roots in 8–12 weeks in a warm propagator or closed case at 64–70°F (18–21°C). It takes 3–5 years to obtain a good-sized plant.
◨–◪◊ min. 55°F/13°C; some **Z9–11**

Cornus
(Dogwood)
Moderately easy to propagate from softwood cuttings taken in late spring or early summer, as for *Acer (see p.61)*. This technique is recommended for variegated cultivars. Pot up cuttings as soon as they have rooted.
◨–◪◊ **Z4–9**

Ficus
(Fig)
Easily propagated. Take 12in (30cm) hardwood cuttings of *F. carica* in late autumn or winter. Root in pots at 50–59°F (10–15°C).

Semi-ripe cuttings of tender evergreens may be taken all year and rooted in a propagating case at 64–70°F (18–21°C). Species with thick stems (e.g. *F. elastica*) can be grown from leaf-bud cuttings – roll the leaf into a cylinder to reduce moisture loss. Keep humid at 68°F (20°C).
◨–◪◊ min. 59°F/15°C; some **Z10–11**

Ilex
(Holly)
Moderately easy. Take hardwood cuttings, 3in (8cm) long, with a basal wound, from autumn to midwinter. Provide bottom heat. Take semi-ripe cuttings, with a basal wound, in late summer to autumn. Both can take three months to root.
Take semi-ripe cuttings of deciduous species in early or midsummer – do not wound. Root semi-ripe cuttings in a cold frame.
◨–◪◊ **Z5–9**

Laburnum
(Golden rain tree)
Easy from 8–12in (20–30cm) long hardwood cuttings in

LABURNUM × WATERERI
'VOSSII'

late autumn. Remove with a heel or at the union of the current and last season's growth. Cutting into pithy tissue of new growth hinders rooting. Root outdoors, lining a trench with coarse sand, or in bundles in a cold frame, then pot in spring.
◨◊ **Z5–8**

Magnolia
Moderately easy. For deciduous species, take softwood cuttings from late spring to early summer, or greenwood cuttings from early to midsummer. Trim all but top two leaves. Root in humid shade with bottom heat of 64–70°F (18–21°C). Fertilize rooted cuttings to ripen them, and overwinter in a frost-free place.
◨–◪◊–◊ **Z3–9**

Morus
(Mulberry)
Moderately easy from 8in (20cm) hardwood cuttings in late autumn. Root them in a sheltered spot outdoors, then lift a year later. Alternatively, take thick pieces of two- to four-year-old wood (truncheons) and root them outdoors – in final positions if desired. This will give larger young plants in a shorter period of time.
◨◊ **Z4–9**

Prunus
(Including cherries and plums)
Hardwood cuttings (12in/30cm) of deciduous species in late autumn are easy but slow. Insert in a sand bed in a cold frame over winter, in bundles of 10. Plant out singly in a nursery bed in spring (they should have rooted).

MAGNOLIA DENUDATA

Semi-ripe cuttings of ever-greens such as *P. lusitanica* are moderately easy from early to midautumn in a temperature of 68°F (20°C).
☑◊ **Z3–10**

Robinia
(Locust)
Moderately easy from root cuttings taken from late autumn to early winter. Choose roots about ½in (1cm) in diameter, but do not wash them. Cuttings can be 3–6in (8–15cm) in length. Store them vertically in a box of moist sand in a cool, frost-free place. In early spring insert them ½in (1cm) deep in pots of free-draining medium to root at 50°F (10°C). Grow on the young plants in pots.
☑◊ **Z4–10**

Salix
(Willow)
Very easy from hardwood cuttings (8in/20cm) taken from late autumn to early spring. Cuttings of vigorous willows may be as long as 6ft (2m) and planted out immediately to mature faster. Line out in a nursery bed.
☑◊ **Z4–9**

CONIFERS

Mainly evergreen, conifers provide interest all year round and are excellent companions for deciduous trees. Some are also widely used for hedging.

Chamaecyparis
(False cypress)
Easy from semi-ripe cuttings taken from late summer to midautumn. Make them 3–4in (10–15cm) long: the base should not be too woody. Keep humid with bottom heat of about 68°F (20°C) maximum. Rooting may take 6–9 months.
☑◊ **Z3–9**

Cupressus
(Cypress)
Cultivars are moderately easy to propagate from semi-ripe cuttings. For best results take 3–4in (8–10cm) green shoots in late winter, then root them under mist with bottom heat of 68°F (20°C) maximum. Cuttings may also be rooted under cover in late summer.
C. macrocarpa and cultivars are often used for hedging.
☑◊ **Z6–10**

Juniperus
(Juniper)
Moderately easy from semi-ripe cuttings (4in/10cm). In late summer or autumn take strong, juvenile shoots (with needlelike leaves), green at the base. Root in a cold frame (should root within a year). Or, root in late winter with bottom heat.
☑–☑◊ **Z3–10**

Picea
(Spruce)
Challenging. From young plants, choose nearly ripe shoots, with firm but not woody bases. For mid-winter cuttings provide bottom heat of 59–68°F (15–20°C).
☑◊ **Z3–9**

Podocarpus
Easily grown from semi-ripe cuttings in late summer. Can be rooted in a cold frame at that point, or root under mist or plastic film with bottom heat of 68°F (20°C).
☑◊ **Z7–10**

Taxus
(Yew)
Fairly easy from autumn cuttings, 4–6in (10–15cm) long, from one- to three-year-old, upright, nearly ripe shoots, green at the base. Rooting by early summer outdoors; earlier with mist and bottom heat of 68°F (20°C).
☑–☑◊ **Z5–8**

PODOCARPUS NIVALIS

SHRUBS AND CLIMBERS

MANY OF THE PLANTS USED in creating the permanent framework of planting designs are shrubs, while climbers can provide color and interest at a higher level. When several shrubs are needed to form groups, the majority can be propagated from cuttings – and the same is true of climbers.

Argyranthemum
Easily raised shrubs. Usually propagated annually for summer bedding from semi-ripe cuttings taken from non-flowering shoots in late summer. Root with gentle bottom heat, 59°F (15°C), in airy conditions. Then transfer to 3½in (9cm) pots of potting mix and winter in a cool, frost-free greenhouse.
⌾◊ **Z10–11**

Aucuba japonica
Easily propagated shrub. In late summer root semi-ripe cuttings in a sheltered nursery bed, such as a cold frame or under covers. Alternatively, bottom heat at 70°F (21°C) speeds up rooting, which will take around 6–8 weeks. Leave cuttings until spring before potting. Plants in 3–4 years.
⌾–◧–▨◊ **Z6–10**

ARGYRANTHEMUM
'JAMAICA PRIMROSE'

Berberis
(Barberry)
Moderately easy shrubs. Take semi-ripe cuttings from mid-summer, or mallet cuttings in early summer (deciduous species) or autumn (evergreens). Take evergreen hardwood cuttings from late autumn to midwinter. Root in cold frames; use bottom heat for deciduous mallet cuttings.
⌾◊ **Z3–9**

Bougainvillea
Climbers, moderately easy to propagate. Softwood or semi-ripe cuttings (2–3in/5–8cm) in summer, taken with a heel, will root in 4–6 weeks if kept humid with bottom heat of 59°F (15°C). In winter root hardwood cuttings (8in/20cm) in deep pots with bottom heat of 70°F (21°C).
⌾◊ **Z9–11**

Buddleja
(Butterfly bush)
Easily propagated shrubs. Hardwood cuttings (8in/20cm) are simplest, taken from autumn to midwinter. Insert in deep pots and place in a cool greenhouse over winter. Plant out the following spring.
⌾◊ **Z6–9**

Callistemon
(Bottlebrush)
Easily propagated shrubs needing acidic to neutral soil. Root greenwood to semi-ripe

cuttings, prepared from side shoots, in summer and autumn. Take with a heel to aid rooting. Cuttings root well in rockwool cells. Provide steady bottom heat; 70°F (21°C) is ideal.
⌾◊ **Z8–11**

Camellia
Acidic soil-loving shrubs, moderately easy to propagate from semi-ripe cuttings between midsummer and early autumn. They may be internodal or nodal leaf-bud cuttings with a ⅝in (1.5cm) basal wound, or nodal tip cuttings. Root in humid conditions with bottom heat of 68°F (20°C).
◧◊ **Z6–8**

Campsis
(Trumpet vine)
Climbers. Easy to raise from hardwood cuttings (8in/20cm) taken between autumn and midwinter. Keep them cool and humid, such as in a cool greenhouse. Also easy from root cuttings (2in/5cm) in winter – they will root in a cold frame but respond more quickly in a frost-free greenhouse.
⌾◊ **Z5–9**

Caryopteris
(Bluebeard)
Easily propagated shrubs. Softwood cuttings from spring to midsummer and

CHOISYA TERNATA

greenwood cuttings from late spring to midsummer. In a warm humid environment under glass, rooting occurs within three weeks. Semi-ripe cuttings from mid- to late summer, as above or in a cold frame. Hardwood cuttings (8in/20cm) from late autumn to midwinter, in pots with gentle bottom heat.
◙◊ Z6–9

Ceanothus
(California lilac)
Shrubs, moderately easy to grow from cuttings. Grow deciduous shrubs from softwood cuttings, taken in late spring to midsummer, with bottom heat of 59°F (15°C). Grow evergreens from semi-ripe cuttings with a heel, taken from midsummer to late autumn, as above. Pot root cuttings (2in/5cm) in autumn; place in frost-free greenhouse.
◙◊ Z7–10

Chaenomeles
These shrubs are easily raised from hardwood cuttings, 8in (20cm) long, taken from autumn to midwinter. Wound the base of each cutting, then

root in pots in a cool greenhouse. Root cuttings taken from autumn to mid-winter are also easy, each about 3in (8cm) long and ⅓in (8mm) in diameter. Lay horizontally on the medium surface and lightly cover. Root in a frost-free greenhouse.
◙–◙◊ Z5–9

Choisya
Easily propagated shrubs. Take greenwood cuttings in midsummer and root in a propagator with bottom heat of 59°F (15°C). Take evergreen hardwood cuttings from late autumn to late winter, 8–10in (20–25cm) or 4in (10cm) long. Root in a frost-free green-house with humidity. Pot when rooted. In mild areas root under covers; transplant the following autumn.
◙◊ Z8–10

Cistus
These shrubs are easily raised from semi-ripe cuttings taken from midsummer to autumn. They can be rooted in a cold frame. Expect good results from cuttings taken in mid-autumn and rooted under a tunnel cover, especially in mild areas. Transplant the following autumn when plants are well rooted.
◙◊ Z8–10

Clematis
These climbers are easily raised from leaf-bud cuttings taken from spring to late summer. Prepare the cuttings from soft or semi-ripe shoots. Root in warm, humid conditions with bottom heat of 59°F (15°C). Semi-ripe cuttings need less humidity. Pot when well rooted (spring

COTONEASTER FRIGIDUS 'CORNUBIA'

for semi-ripe cuttings). Keep young plants in sheltered conditions.
◙◊ Z4–9

Cornus
(Dogwood)
These shrubs, grown for their colored stems, are easily propagated from hardwood cuttings (8in/20cm) taken late autumn to midwinter. Root in a sheltered site, ideally in cold frames. If necessary, keep well watered during the growing season. The frames can be opened fully in the spring. Transplant rooted cuttings the following autumn.
◙◊–◊ Z2–8

Cotoneaster
These shrubs are easily propagated from cuttings. Take softwood or greenwood cuttings from spring to mid-summer, then root them in a propagating case with bottom heat of 59°F (15°C). Pot as soon as rooted. Alternatively, take semi-ripe cuttings from midsummer to autumn and root in cold frames or, in mild areas, under covers.
◙◊ Z5–9

Cytisus

These shrubs are moderately easy to propagate. Take semi-ripe cuttings in late summer or early autumn, with or without a heel. Use a free-draining medium or rockwool cubes. Providing humidity and bottom heat of 54–59°F (12–15°C) speeds rooting.
◫◊ Z6–9

Daphne

Moderately easy shrubs to propagate. Take stem-tip greenwood cuttings from spring to early summer, or stem-tip semi-ripe cuttings in summer. Provide bottom heat of 59°F (15°C) for both.
◫–◫◊ Z5–9

Elaeagnus

Moderately easy shrubs to propagate. Take semi-ripe cuttings from late summer to autumn. Wound at the base ¾in (2cm). Bottom heat at 59–68°F (15–20°C) speeds rooting. Alternatively, take hardwood cuttings of vigorous growth from late autumn to late winter. Root in frost-free, humid conditions.
◫–◫◊ Z2–10

ERICA CARNEA
'VIVELLII'

FATSIA JAPONICA

Erica
(Heath)

Most of these shrubs require acidic soil. Easily propagated from semi-ripe cuttings of nonflowering sideshoots in summer. Insert in cell packs, then root in a propagator at 59–70°F (15–21°C). Pot when well rooted.
◫◊ Z5–11

Escallonia

Easy shrubs to propagate. Take greenwood or semi-ripe cuttings from midsummer to autumn. Root greenwood cuttings with bottom heat, 59°F (15°C), semi-ripe in a cold frame. Root evergreen hardwood cuttings, 8–10in (20–25cm) long, from late autumn to late winter, in a frost-free environment.
◫◊ Z7–9

Euonymus
(Burning bush, Spindle)

Easy shrubs to propagate. Take softwood or semi-ripe cuttings, in spring to late summer; greenwood cuttings in late spring for *Euonymus alatus*; with bottom heat of 59°F (15°C).
◫–◫◊ Z2–9

Fatsia japonica

This shrub is easily raised from cuttings. Take semi-ripe tip cuttings 3–4in (8–10cm) in length, at any time. Remove all but the top two leaves. Insert cuttings so that only the bottom leaf joints are buried. Root in a propagator with bottom heat of 59–68°F (15–20°C).
◫–◫◊ Z8–10

Fuchsia

Easily propagated shrubs. Take softwood cuttings at any time: nodal stem-tip, single-node, and internodal stem cuttings all root readily. Take semi-ripe cuttings from mid-summer to early autumn. Root in a propagator with bottom heat of 59°F (15°C).
◫–◫◊ Z7–10

Grevillea

Moderately easy shrubs to propagate. They need acidic soil low in phosphorus. Take semi-ripe heeled cuttings from late summer into autumn. Best results gained with provision of bottom heat of around 59°F (15°C).
◫◊ Z9–11

HEBE × FRANCISCANA
'VARIEGATA'

HEDERA HELIX 'GOLDHEART'
(SYN. 'ORO DI BOGLIASCO')

Hebe

Easily raised shrubs. Take softwood stem-tip cuttings, spring to autumn, for large-leaved species. Provide bottom heat of 59°F (15°C). Semi-ripe stem-tip cuttings for all, midsummer to late autumn.
◧–◪◊ Z8–11

Hedera
(Ivy)
Easily raised climbers and a few shrubs. Take leaf-bud cuttings of soft or semi-ripe shoots from spring to autumn. For bushy plants, use adult growth. Keep shaded.
◪–▦◊ Z5–10

Hydrangea
Easily raised shrubs. Root softwood stem-tip cuttings from late spring to mid-summer, with bottom heat of 59°F (15°C). Rooting takes 2–4 weeks. Root semi-ripe cuttings in midsummer, in a cool place.
◧–◪◊ Z4–9

Hypericum
Easily raised shrubs. Softwood or semi-ripe cuttings from spring to

autumn, softwood cuttings in a propagator with heat, semi-ripe in a cold frame. Hardwood cuttings in pots from late autumn to mid-winter, in a cool greenhouse.
◧–◪◊ Z5–9

Jasminum
(Jasmine)
Easily raised shrubs and climbers. Softwood or semi-ripe cuttings in spring and summer, in a heated propagator and cold frame respectively. Hardwood cuttings (8in/20cm) in winter for *J. nudiflorum* and *J. officinale*, in a cold frame.
◧–◪◊ Z6–11

Lavandula
(Lavender)
Moderately easy shrubs to grow from semi-ripe cuttings with a heel in summer or early autumn. Root in a cold frame or under covers.
◪◊ Z5–10

Lonicera
(Honeysuckle)
Shrubs and climbers are easily grown from cuttings: soft-wood or semi-ripe cuttings rooted with bottom heat from late spring to late summer; hardwood cuttings in a cold frame from late autumn.
◧–◪◊ Z4–10

Mahonia
Easily propagated shrubs. Prepare leaf-bud cuttings with 1–2in (2.5–5cm) of stem, from current year's shoots in autumn. Wound the base, reduce the leaves, and root with humidity and bottom heat of 59–68°F (15–20°C).
◧–◪–▦◊ Z6–10

LAVANDULA ANGUSTIFOLIA
'TWICKEL PURPLE'

Passiflora
(Passionflower)
These climbers are easily propagated from leaf-bud cuttings taken from soft or semi-ripe shoots, spring to late summer. Root in cell packs in a humid environment with bottom heat of 68°F (20°C). Overwinter under cover.
◧–◪◊ Z6–11

Philadelphus
(Mock orange)
Easily raised shrubs. Take softwood cuttings from late spring and root in a propagator or similar environment with bottom heat of 59°F (15°C). Semi-ripe cuttings (3in/8cm) in summer will root in a cold frame.
◧–◪◊ Z3–9

Philodendron
Shrubs or climbers, often epiphytic, easily propagated at any time from leaf-bud, stem-tip, and stem cuttings, up to 4in (10cm) long, of soft or semi-ripe wood. Rooting takes 4–6 weeks in humid conditions at 70–77°F (21–25°C).
◪◊ min. 59°F/15°C

PYRACANTHA
'ORANGE GLOW'

Pittosporum

These shrubs are moderately
easy from semi-ripe cuttings
in autumn. Place a ¼in (2cm)
layer of coarse sand over the
medium. Rooting takes 8–12
weeks at 54–68°F (12–20°C).
◩–◪◊ Z9–10

Pyracantha

(Firethorn)
These shrubs are easily
propagated from semi-ripe
cuttings from late summer to
early autumn. Root in a cold
frame or, for quicker results,
in a propagator with bottom
heat of 59°F (15°C).
◩–◪◊ Z5–9

Rhododendron

Acidic soil-loving shrubs.
Fairly easy. Softwood cuttings
in spring for deciduous
azaleas, in a humid prop-
agator at 68°F (20°C). Semi-
ripe cuttings midsummer to
autumn for evergreens (same
conditions). Wound bases.
◪◊–◊ Z4–9

Ribes

(Currants and gooseberries)
Ornamental and fruiting
shrubs. Easy from hardwood
cuttings (8in/20cm) in late
autumn or winter. Insert
outdoors, but in a cold frame
for ornamentals.
◩◊ Z2–10

Rosa

Shrubs and climbers. Many
roses are easily propagated
from hardwood cuttings
(8in/20cm) taken in winter,
inserted in a sheltered spot
outdoors.
◩◊ Z2–9

Salvia

Shrubby salvias are easily
propagated from semi-ripe
cuttings taken from side
shoots in late summer or early
autumn. Root in a cold frame
or cool greenhouse.
◩◊ Z7–10

Syringa

(Lilac)
Shrubs, moderately easy from
softwood cuttings in spring.
Root in a propagator with
bottom heat of 59°F (15°C).
◩◊ Z2–8

Thymus

(Thyme)
These shrubs are easy from
2–3in (5–8cm) softwood
cuttings in late spring or
summer. Or take 2in (5cm)
heel cuttings in late spring.
Root in cell packs with
bottom heat of 59°F (15°C).
◩◊ Z4–9

Viburnum

Shrubs. Evergreens are fairly
easy from semi-ripe cuttings,
late summer or autumn, with
some bottom heat. Deciduous
species from hardwood
cuttings (8in/20cm) in winter,
placed in a cold frame.
◩–◪◊ Z4–10

Vitis

(Table grapes and
ornamental grapes)
Climbers, easily grown from
hardwood cuttings taken in
winter, with bottom heat of
70°F (21°C). Root standard
hardwood cuttings in deep
pots. Alternatively, prepare
vine eyes consisting of a
single bud, then insert them
in cell packs.
◩–◪◊ Z4–10

Wisteria

These climbers are easily
propagated. Softwood
cuttings in late spring to
midsummer with bottom
heat of 59°F (15°C). Hardwood cuttings (8in/20cm)
in winter in a frost-free
greenhouse. Root them
with bottom heat.
◩–◪◊ Z5–9

Yucca

Shrubs. Easy from leafless
stem sections. Prepare 4in
(10cm) cuttings from a
mature stem. Insert single
cuttings vertically into 3½in
(9cm) pots. Keep humid at
70–75°F (21–24°C).
◩◊ Z5–10

VITIS COIGNETIAE

PERENNIALS

Nonwoody plants, or perennials, form a group of enormous value. They include border plants, rock plants or alpines, aquatics, and, in frost-prone climates, tender plants for summer bedding and greenhouse display. While division is a major method of propagation, many are easily raised from cuttings.

Acanthus
(Bear's breeches)
Architectural plants, easily propagated from root cuttings taken during mid- to late autumn. Lift the entire plant and wash roots free of soil. Choose roots of medium thickness. Cut into 2–4in (5–10cm) sections, making thinner cuttings the longest. Insert vertically in pots and cover with ½in (1cm) layer of grit. Root in a cold frame or propagator. Pot in spring.
◙–◙◊ Z5–11

Achillea
(Yarrow)
Easily propagated herbaceous plants. Basal stem cuttings taken in spring will flower within a year. Root in a propagating case with gentle bottom heat of 59–64°F (15–18°C). Semi-ripe stem-tip cuttings taken in early autumn can be rooted in a cool greenhouse or cold frame, potted into small pots when well rooted and overwintered in a cold frame.
◙◊ Z3–9

Anemone
(Windflower)
Root cuttings offer the easiest means of increasing clumps of fleshy-rooted anemones. Take cuttings in autumn or winter by lifting the edge of a clump – do not take the entire plant. Root them in a cold frame and pot up when rooted. They usually flower in 2–3 years.
◙–◙◊ Z4–9

Artemisia
(Wormwood)
These herbaceous or woody-based perennials are fairly easy to grow from cuttings. Take stem tips or heeled sideshoots as greenwood cuttings in late summer. (*A. absinthium* 'Lambrook Silver' roots best from softwood cuttings in spring.) Root in a propagating case with bottom heat of 64–70°F (18–21°C).
◙◊ Z3–9

Aster
Easily propagated herbaceous perennials. Take basal stem cuttings in spring and root in a propagator or under mist

ARTEMISIA LUDOVICIANA

with bottom heat of 64–70°F (18–21°C). Pot up and grow on in a cold frame.
◙–◙◊ Z3–8

Aubrieta
(Aubretia)
Easy-to-grow mat- or mound-forming plants. Take fully ripe cuttings in late summer or early autumn when shoots are mature. Root in a cold frame.
◙◊ Z5–7

Begonia
A diverse genus of perennials. Stem-tip cuttings of stem-forming species, in spring or autumn, are easy, as are leaf cuttings in spring or summer of *B. rex*, *B. masoniana*, and similar types. Use whole leaves or cut leaf into squares. Root in humid conditions at 70°F (21°C).
◙◊ min. 41–55°F/5–13°C

ASTER AMELLUS
'KING GEORGE'

BERGENIA 'SUNNINGDALE'

Bergenia
(Elephant's ears)
These rhizomatous perennials are easy from leafless rhizome cuttings taken from mature plants in autumn. Wash the rhizomes free of soil and trim back any long roots. Cut rhizome into 1½–2in (4–5cm) sections, each with several dormant buds, half bury in moist perlite (buds uppermost), and root in humid conditions with bottom heat of 70°F (21°C). Pot up when rooted, then grow on in a cold frame. Flowers in 1–2 years.
▣–▨◊ Z3–8

Campanula
(Bellflower)
Herbaceous plants, some good for rock gardens, moderately easy to propagate from cuttings. Basal stem cuttings of rock-garden types taken in late spring root in 2–3 weeks in a cold frame. Take stem-tip cuttings of herbaceous border species from new growth after flowering, then root in a propagator with bottom heat of 64–70°F (18–21°C).
▣–▨◊ Z3–9

Chrysanthemum
Florists' chrysanthemums are easily propagated from basal stem cuttings in spring, generally taken from stock plants wintered under cover, or direct from garden plants. Root in propagator with bottom heat of 50°F (10°C). Pot when rooted, grow on in a heated greenhouse, and plant out or pot on in late spring.
▣◊ Z5–8

Dahlia
These tuberous perennials are easily propagated in spring from stock plants wintered in the dormant state under cover. Start plants into growth in early spring by increasing warmth and moisture and take basal stem cuttings when ready. Root at about 66°F (19°C) in humid conditions. Pot up, harden off in a cold frame. Plant out after frosts.
▣◊ Z8–10

Delphinium
These border perennials are easily propagated from basal stem cuttings taken in late spring. Root them in pots of perlite (stand pot in a saucer of water) at 59°F (15°C) and pot as soon as rooted. Alternatively, do in rooting medium. Harden off and plant out in early summer.
▣◊ Z3–7

Dendrobium
(Orchid)
Take leafless stem cuttings in spring. Remove a 10in (25cm) long section of stem (cut just above a leaf joint). Divide it into 3in/8cm long sections, each with at least one joint, cutting between nodes. Lay cuttings on moist sphagnum

DELPHINIUM 'BRUCE'

moss, cover, and root in warm, humid conditions. Cuttings should produce plantlets in a few weeks.
▨◊ min. 50–55°F/10–13°C

Dianthus
(Carnation, pink)
The perennial members of this diverse genus range from border and rock plants to perpetual-flowering carnations. All are easily propagated from semi-ripe cuttings, known as pipings, from mid- to late summer. Just snap them off. Root them in a cold frame, or in a propagating case with bottom heat of 59°F (15°C).
▣◊ Z3–8

Diascia
These perennials are easily raised from softwood stem-tip cuttings in spring, or from the regrowth on plants trimmed after flowering in late summer. Root in a propagator with bottom heat of 64–70°F (18–21°C). Overwinter late-rooted cuttings in a cool greenhouse, then plant out the following spring.
▣◊ Z7–9

DIEFFENBACHIA
'EXOTICA'

Dieffenbachia
(Dumb cane)
Evergreen perennial, fairly
easy from leafless stem
sections in spring. Cut stem
into 2in (5cm) pieces, cutting
each below a leaf joint. Press
flat into rooting medium,
buds uppermost, and root in
humid conditions at 70°F
(21°C). Sap is toxic.
◼◊ min. 59°F/15°C

Epimedium
(Barrenwort)
These rhizomatous woodland-
garden perennials are easy to
grow from rhizome cuttings

ERYNGIUM ALPINUM

EUPHORBIA POLYCHROMA

taken in winter. Lift a clump
and wash off the soil. Cut off
the old leaves. Separate
individual rhizomes, cut them
into 2–3in (5–8cm) sections,
then treat them as root
cuttings. Lay on medium
surface, cover with ½in
(12mm) of medium, and place
in a cold frame. Pot up when
growth starts in spring.
◼◊ Z4–9

Eryngium
(Sea holly)
Border perennials, moderately
easy from root cuttings in late
autumn. Take cuttings from
thick roots; cut into 2–3in
(5–8cm) pieces. Lay flat on
trays of medium, cover with
medium, and root in a frost-
free greenhouse. Pot singly in
spring when shoots appear.
Harden off in a cold frame,
plant out when established.
◼◊ Z3–9

Euphorbia
(Spurge)
The border perennials in this
varied genus are moderately
easy from summer or autumn
cuttings. Take stem-tip
cuttings from mature growth

after flowering, making them
2–4in (5–10cm) long. Allow
to stand for an hour for the
sap to dry. Root in a cold
frame. Excess humidity can
cause rot. Pot when rooted;
plant out in spring.
◼–◼◊–◊ Z4–10

Geranium
(Cranesbill)
These herbaceous perennials
are easy from root cuttings,
especially *G. pratense*, *G.
phaeum*, and *G. sanguineum*.
Take 1in (2.5cm) long
cuttings in autumn and root
in a cold frame. Root basal
stem cuttings in spring at
59°F (15°C).
◼–◼◊ Z4–9

Impatiens
(Balsam, Busy Lizzie)
These easily propagated
perennials are often used as
greenhouse pot plants and
summer bedding plants in
frost-prone climates. Take soft
stem-tip cuttings in spring or
summer and root in humid
conditions at 64–70°F
(18–21°C). They will root
even in water.
◼◊ min. 41–50°F/5–10°C

IMPATIENS
NEW GUINEA GROUP

Lewisia
(Bitterroot)
Perennials needing acidic to neutral soil. Rosette cuttings in summer are moderately easy. Remove each offset with some stem and root in a shaded propagator or cold frame. Leaf cuttings in summer are more challenging. Use whole leaves and root in the same conditions.
◨–◪◊ Z3–8

Lobelia
Take stem tip or stem cuttings from border perennials in summer. Moderately easy to root with bottom heat of 64°F (18°C). Flowering stems of Lobelia siphilitica, L. cardinalis, and similar can be cut into 2in (5cm) lengths; remove lower leaves. For more plants, split cuttings vertically, retaining leaves on each half. Protect plants from cold over the winter months.
◨–◪◊ Z3–10

Lupinus
(Lupine)
These perennials are moderately easy from basal stem cuttings in spring. At a

LOBELIA × GERARDII
'VEDRARIENSIS'

LUPINUS
'CHATELAINE'

temperature of 59°F (15°C), rooting takes 10–14 days. To avoid rotting, insert cuttings in perlite. Pot when rooted and grow on in a cold frame or under covers. Plant young lupines out in early summer in slightly acidic soil.
◨–◪◊ Z5–9

Mentha
(Mint)
These herbs are moderately easy from softwood cuttings in summer, rooted with bottom heat of 68°F (20°C). Easier are 1½–3in (4–8cm) rhizome cuttings in spring. Insert vertically and cover with ¼in (5mm) of medium. Keep at 50°F (10°C). Pot up singly when rooted and keep warm until established, then harden off and plant out.
◨–◪◊ Z3–9

Monarda
(Bee balm)
These border perennials are easy to grow from basal stem cuttings taken in spring and given bottom heat of 64–70°F (18–21°C). Alternatively, take soft stem-tip cuttings in spring and root in same conditions.

Pot up as soon as they have rooted, then allow to establish before hardening off in a cold frame prior to planting out.
◨–◪◊ Z4–9

Nymphaea
(Waterlily)
Easily grown from root-bud cuttings (rounded swellings with shoots on the roots) in spring or early summer. Cut out a bud, fill a 4in (10cm) aquatic container with aquatic medium, then press in the bud so tip is still visible. Immerse so bud is just below water level. Overwinter in a frost-free greenhouse.
◨ Z4–11

Oenothera
Easily propagated herbaceous perennials. Take softwood tip cuttings or basal stem cuttings, especially of tap-rooted species (which resent root disturbance), in spring, then root them in a heated propagating case with bottom heat of 64–70°F (18–21°C). Once they have rooted, pot individually and allow to become established under glass before hardening

MONARDA
'CAMBRIDGE SCARLET'

off in a cold frame or similar protected site, prior to planting out.
🔲◊ Z3–10

Osteospermum

These plants are generally used for summer bedding in frost-prone climates and propagated annually. They are easily grown from softwood cuttings in spring with bottom heat of 64–70°F (18–21°C). However, for bedding they are usually propagated from semi-ripe cuttings in late summer, with bottom heat or in a cold frame, and wintered under cover.
🔲◊ Z10–11

Papaver
(Poppy)

Oriental poppies (*Papaver orientalis* cultivars) are easily grown from root cuttings in late autumn. Take cuttings about 3in (8cm) long and insert vertically into rooting medium. Keep in a cold frame or under covers over winter. When well rooted in spring, line out in a nursery bed or pot singly.
🔲◊ Z4–9

PHLOX PANICULATA 'EVENTIDE'

PENSTEMON 'SOUR GRAPES'

Pelargonium

Zonal, regal, and ivy- and scented-leaved geraniums are easily raised from semi-ripe cuttings taken in late summer and given bottom heat of 59°F (15°C), or rooted in a cold frame, and wintered under cover.
🔲◊ min. 36°F/2°C

Penstemon
(Beard tongue)

The border perennials and rock-garden types are easily raised from semi-ripe stem-tip cuttings taken in late summer or early autumn. The cuttings should root in two weeks at a temperature of 59°F (15°C). Protect rooted cuttings during their first winter by keeping them in a cool greenhouse or cold frame.
🔲◊ Z3–10

Phlox

These plants are easily propagated from cuttings. Increase rock garden and woodland species by taking basal stem cuttings in spring. Alternatively, take softwood stem-tip cuttings in spring. Root both kinds of cutting at

PRIMULA DENTICULATA VAR. ALBA

59°F (15°C). Raise border phlox (*Phlox paniculata*) by taking root cuttings in autumn. Aerial parts of border phlox are prone to nematode infestation, but roots are free of this pest. Lay the 1in (2.5cm) cuttings horizontally and cover with ½in (12mm) of medium. Root cuttings in a cold frame.
🔲–🔲◊ Z3–9

Potamogeton
(Curled pondweed)

These aquatic perennials are cultivated as oxygenators in garden pools, particularly *Potamogeton crispus*, and are easy to propagate. Regularly replace this fast-growing plant with young stock propagated from cuttings. Take stem-tip cuttings in late spring or early summer. Tie them loosely in bunches of six and plant in containers of aquatic-plant potting mix.
🔲–🔲 Z7–11

Primula
(Drumstick primrose)

Primula denticulata and its color forms are moderately easily grown from root

RUDBECKIA
'GOLDSTURM'

cuttings in winter. Cut thicker roots into 1½–2in (4–5cm) pieces. Lay them flat on the surface of medium and cover with ½in (12mm) of medium. Root in a cold frame. When well rooted in spring, pot singly or line out in a shady nursery bed to grow on. They should flower in two years.
▨◊ Z2–8

Rudbeckia
(Coneflower)
These border perennials are easily propagated from basal stem cuttings, taken as soon as they become available in spring. Insert in pots or cell packs, then root them in a propagating case with bottom heat of 64–70°F (18–21°C). When rooted, pot individually, allow to become established, then harden off thoroughly in a cold frame prior to planting out. The young plants may flower in the following year.
◫–▨◊ Z3–9

Saintpaulia
(African violet)
Grown as pot plants in frost-prone climates. Easy to

propagate from leaf cuttings in spring or at any time when plants are in growth. Take fully developed, new leaves with their stalks (petioles) as cuttings. Insert in pots, either singly or several around the edge. Root in humid conditions with bottom heat of 70°F (21°C). Pot plantlets individually when they are large enough to handle.
▨◊ min. 64°F/18°C

Salvia
(Sage)
These border perennials are easy to grow from basal stem cuttings in late spring. Root at 59°F (15°C) to flower in the same year. Also easy from soft and semi-ripe stem-tip cuttings from new, non-flowering growth in summer or early autumn. Root in the same way.
◫–▨◊ Z5–10

Sansevieria
(Snake plant)
Grown as pot plants in frost-prone climates. Moderately easy to propagate from leaf cuttings taken at any time

SOLENOSTEMON
WIZARD SERIES

VERBASCUM
'COTSWOLD QUEEN'

of year. (However, note that offspring from variegated cultivars will lack variegation if they are raised from leaf cuttings.) Use newly mature leaves and cut horizontally into 2in (5cm) sections. Insert vertically to half their depth, lower edge downward, in a tray of medium. Root with bottom heat of 70°F (21°C) and avoid humid conditions.
▨◊ min. 55°F/13°C

Solenostemon
(Coleus)
These perennials are grown as pot plants or summer bedding plants in frost-prone climates and are easily raised from cuttings, ideally annually, since young plants have the most vigorous and colorful foliage. Take softwood stem-tip cuttings from early spring to late summer. They root readily in a free-draining medium such as perlite, or even simply in a jar of water on a warm windowsill. They should root in 10–14 days at 64°F (18°C). Pot up as soon as the cuttings have rooted.
◫–▨◊ min. 50°F/10°C

Streptocarpus
(Cape primrose)
These perennials are grown as pot plants in frost-prone climates. Easily raised from leaf cuttings from spring to autumn. Cut a mature leaf in half along the midrib (discard the midrib itself) and insert shallowly, cut side down (*see p.43*). Alternatively, cut leaf into transverse sections or chevrons 5in (2.5cm) deep. Insert, basal end down, in a tray. Root with bottom heat of 64°F (18°C). Keep humid.
▨◊ min. 50°F/10°C

Verbascum
Short-lived border perennials that can easily be increased from root cuttings in late autumn. Lift a vigorous plant, then cut the thicker roots into 2in (5cm) sections. Discard the parent plant. Lay the cuttings flat on a tray of medium and cover with ½in (12mm) of medium. Place in a cold frame or, in colder climates, in a frost-free greenhouse. Pot individually when rooted in spring.
▨◊ Z3–9

Viola
(Pansy, violet)
These short-lived perennials root well from 1–2in (2.5–5cm) stem-tip cuttings in spring, prepared from new shoots before they elongate and become hollow. They root within 14 days at 59°F (15°C). Pot singly when rooted. Alternatively, three weeks before taking autumn cuttings, cut back plants; take stem-tip cuttings from the regrowth. Keep the young plants frost-free over winter.
▨–▨◊ Z2–9

ROSETTE-FORMING ROCK PLANTS

Androsace
(Rock jasmine)
Short-stemmed rosette cuttings in late spring and summer for small, cushion-forming species. Insert in pots of finely ground pumice or horticultural sand. Only the short stem is buried. Root at 50–59°F (10–15°C) in an unheated propagator or cold frame; keep shaded. Gentle bottom heat speeds rooting.
▨◊ Z4–8

Dionysia
These alpines are very difficult to root, being prone to rotting off, especially species like *D. curviflora, D. × tapetodes*, and *D. freitagii*. Take rosette cuttings as for androsace. Remove with ¼–½in (5–10mm) of stem. Use hormone rooting powder.
▨◊ Z5–7

Draba
(Whitlow grass)
Cushion-forming alpines propagated from rosette cuttings as for androsace.
D. rigida var. *bryoides* and *D. mollissima* benefit from rooting in freely draining ground pumice to help prevent rotting off.
▨◊ Z4–6

Morisia
Morisia monanthos is a rosette-forming, taprooted alpine grown from root cuttings in late autumn and winter (moderately easy). Insert cuttings vertically in pure coarse sand, cover with ½in (1cm) layer of grit, and root them in a cold frame. Keep only slightly moist.
▨◊ Z7–9

Saxifraga
(Saxifrage)
This is a large and varied genus, but the small cushion types, such as *S. cebennensis, S. oppositifolia*, and *S. poluniniana*, are propagated from rosette cuttings as for androsace, and are best inserted in ground pumice.
▨–▨◊ Z1–10

ANDROSACE VANDELLII

DRABA MOLLISSIMA

CACTI AND SUCCULENTS

Taking cuttings offers a reliable way of increasing many succulent plants. Use semi-ripe or ripe material. Root the cuttings in a mix of two parts cactus potting mix and one part coarse sand, with a top-dressing of coarse sand to prevent cuttings from rotting. Insert shallowly to avoid rot (*see also p.42*).

Aeonium
Tall species easily propagated from large, callused stem cuttings, in spring or early autumn. Cut stem 3–12in (8–30cm) below rosette. Pot individually, 2–3in (5–8cm) deep. Rosette cuttings for smaller species. Root with bottom heat of 70°F (21°C).
◙◊ min. 41°F/5°C

Aloe
Easily propagated from leaf cuttings in spring and summer. Use whole leaves from halfway up the plant, and set them in individual small pots. Root them in about 64°F (18°C).
◙◊ min. 50°F/10°C

Cephalocereus
(Old man cactus)
Moderately easy from cuttings, spring or summer,

Aloe aristata

but only to save a plant that has rotted at the base. Take a large stem cutting from top of plant, allow it to callus, and insert in an individual pot. Root with bottom heat of 64–75°F (18–24°C).
◙◊ min. 50°F/10°C

Cereus
These columnar cacti are moderately easy from stem cuttings in spring or summer. Cuttings up to 6ft (2m) long can be taken but are generally shorter. Stand cutting on layer of fine gravel when potting. It may need support. Otherwise as for cephalocereus.
◙◊ min. 41°F/5°C

Crassula
Easy from 2–4in (5–10cm) stem cuttings in spring or summer. Moderately easy from leaf cuttings in spring or summer, but slow. Use entire leaves and insert upright. Allow both to callus and root with bottom heat of 64–70°F (18–21°C).
◙◊ min. 41–50°F/5–10°C

Echeveria
Propagated from leaf cuttings in spring or summer. Moderately easy. Take whole leaves from main stem near base of rosette, then insert upright after allowing to callus. Root with bottom heat of 64°F (18°C).
◙◊ min. 45°F/7°C

Echinopsis
Globular species and *E. chamaecereus* are easily propagated from the offsets, which fall away. Use these as stem cuttings in spring or summer. Root with bottom heat of 70°F (21°C).
◙◊ min. 41–50°F/5–10°C

Epiphyllum
(Orchid cactus)
These epiphytic forest cacti are easy from flat stem cuttings taken from spring to late summer. Cut stems into 6–9in (15–23cm) lengths. Allow to callus, then insert upright. Root at 64–75°F (18–24°C) in humid conditions.
◙◊ min. 50°F/10°C

Euphorbia
(Spurge)
Stem-producing species such as *E. milii* and *E. canariensis* are moderately easy from well-callused stem cuttings, mid-spring to summer. Root with bottom heat of 70°F (21°C).
◙◊ min. 45–59°F/7–15°C

Haworthia
Moderately easy from cuttings, spring to autumn. Use severed offsets of taller species as stem cuttings. Leaf cuttings (whole leaves) for non-offsetting plants, but these are very slow to root. Root all with bottom heat of 64–70°F (18–21°C).
◙–◙◊ min. 50°F/10°C

Hoya
(Wax flower)
Moderately easy to propagate from stem cuttings taken in spring or summer. Cut a length of stem just below a node and 3–4 nodes long. Dip base in hormone rooting powder. Root with bottom heat of 70°F (21°C). Rooting takes 2–6 weeks.
▣◊ min. 45–55°F/7–13°C

Kalanchoe
Easily propagated from stem or leaf cuttings in spring or summer. Take stem cuttings after flowering. Use whole leaves complete with stalk (petiole) and insert upright. Allow all cuttings to callus for 24 hours before inserting them. Root with bottom heat of 64–70°F (18–21°C).
▣–▣◊ min. 50–54°F/10–12°C

Lithops
(Living stones)
Cuttings in early summer are moderately easy to grow. Remove offsets of one or more heads from larger clumps, then treat as globular stem cuttings. Allow to callus well. They are prone to rotting, so be prepared for losses. Root with bottom heat of 70°F (21°C).
▣◊ min. 54°F/12°C

Mammillaria
(Pincushion cactus)
Moderately easy to propagate from spring or summer cuttings. Remove offsets and use them as globular stem cuttings. Some offsets can be pulled away easily; others will require a knife. Root with bottom heat of 70°F (21°C).
▣◊ min. 45–50°F/7–10°C

OPUNTIA MICRODASYS VAR. ALBISPINA

Opuntia
(Prickly pear)
These cacti are easy to grow from cuttings taken in spring or summer. Remove single pads as stem cuttings, cutting them off at a joint. Allow to callus for three days. Bottom heat of 66°F (19°C).
▣◊ min. 45–50°F/7–10°C; some hardy Z6–11

Rebutia
These cacti are easy from cuttings in spring or summer. Sever offsets at their bases and use as globular stem cuttings. Allow to callus for 2–3 days, then root with bottom heat of 70°F (21°C).
▣◊ min. 41–45°F/5–7°C

Rhipsalis
(Mistletoe cactus)
These epiphytic forest cacti are easily propagated from stem cuttings in spring or summer. Detach a slender stem at a joint and cut it into 4–6in (10–15cm) long sections. Then treat as for epiphyllum cuttings. The cuttings should root in 3–6 weeks.
▣◊ min. 50°F/10°C

SCHLUMBERGERA 'SPECTABILE COCCINEUM'

Schlumbergera
(Christmas cactus)
Epiphytic forest cacti, easily raised from flat stem cuttings, 2–3 segments long. Treat as for epiphyllum cuttings. Root two or more cuttings back to back in a pot for fuller pots of plants.
▣◊ min. 50°F/10°C

Sedum
(Stonecrop)
Easy from cuttings in spring or summer. Tender and hardy species from whole-leaf, stem-tip, or rosette cuttings. Allow to callus for a day. Leaf cuttings can be rooted on damp newspaper. Bottom heat of 70°F (21°C) for all.
▣◊ min. 41°F/5°C, many hardy Z3–10

Sempervivum
(Houseleek)
Easy from cuttings in summer. Unrooted offsets can be severed at the base of their stem and used as rosette cuttings. Rosettes sit on medium surface with stem buried. Root with bottom heat of 70°F (21°C).
▣◊ Z4–10

INDEX

Page numbers in **bold italics** refer to illustrated information

A
Abelia **29**
Acanthus 9, **9**, **44**, 69
Acer 30, 61, **61**
Achillea 69
adventitious roots 14, **14–15**
Aeonium 76
Ailanthus **29**, 61
Aloe 76, **76**
alpines 46, 75
Androsace 75, **75**
Anemone **19**, 69
aphids **59**
Argyranthemum **64**, **64**
Artemisia 69, **69**
asparagus 45
Aster 38, 69, **69**
Aubrieta 69
Aucuba **32**, 64
azaleas 16, 23

B
bark **26**
basal stem cuttings **29**, 38–39, **38–39**
Begonia **9**, 43, **43**, 69
Berberis 35, **35**, 64
Bergenia 45, **45**, 70, **70**
Betula 30, 61
blackleg **55**
blankets, propagating **12**
Bougainvillea 64
Buddleja 64

C
cacti 20–1, 46, 47, **47**, 76–77
Callistemon 64
Calluna 33, **33**
callus tissue **15**, 54
Camellia **17**, 33, **33**, 40, **40**, 64
Campanula 70
Campsis 64

Caryopteris 64–65
Ceanothus **29**, 35, **35**, 65
cell trays 25, **25**
Cephalocereus 76
Cereus **47**, 76
Chaenomeles 65
Chamaecyparis **17**, **34**, 63
chamomile 18
chevron leaf cuttings **29**
Choisya 65, **65**
chrysanthemums 38, 70
Cistus 65
Clematis **7**, 9, **29**, 40, **40**, 65
climbers 16, 23, 64–68
    hardwood cuttings 36
    leaf-bud cuttings 40–41
    semi-ripe cuttings 32
    softwood cuttings 30
cloches/covers 11, **49**, 52, **52**
clonal propagation 9
coir **26**
cold damage **59**
cold frames 11, 49, 52, 53, **53**, 57, **57**
Columnea 9
conifers 16, 34, **34**, 63
Cordyline 46, 62, **62**
Cornus 62, 65
Cotoneaster **29**, 65, **65**
Crassula **20**, 42, 76
Cupressus 63
cutworms **59**
Cytisus 66

D
Daboecia 33
Dahlia 70
damping off 27, 55
Daphne 66
Delphinium **29**, 39, 70, **70**
Dendrobium 70
Dianthus **19**, 34, **34**, 70
Diascia 39, 70
Dieffenbachia 46, 71, **71**

Dionysia **46**, 75
diseases 13, 55, **59**
Draba 75, **75**
Dracaena fragrans 40

E
Echeveria 42, **47**, 76
Echinopsis 76
Elaeagnus 66
Elymus 45
Epimedium 71
Epiphyllum **21**, **47**, **47**, 76
Erica 33, 66, **66**
Eryngium 71, **71**
Escallonia 66
Euonymus 66
Euphorbia 71, **71**, 76
evergreens 32, 36

F
Fatsia **29**, 66, **66**
Ficus 40, 62
florist's foam **27**
fog propagation 12, **13**, 56
Forsythia 36
Fuchsia **6**, 66
fungal diseases 49, 55, **59**
fungicides 28, **28**

G
Geranium 71
grapes 37, **37**
greenhouses 11, **11**, **48**, 50, **50–52**, 54, **54**, 55
greenwood cuttings 30
Grevillea 66
gray mold **55**

H
hardening off 57
hardwood cuttings 9, 17, 23, **29**, 36–37, **36–37**
Haworthia 76
heathers 33, **33**, 56, **56**
Hebe **23**, 66, 67

Hedera 14, 29, 40, *41*, 67, *67*
heel cuttings *15*, *29*, 35, *35*
herbs 45, *45*
hormone rooting powder 28, *28*
horseradish 45, *45*
hot beds 11, *11*
Hoya 9, 77
humidity 49, *50*, 54, 56
Hydrangea 9, *31*, 67
hygiene 25, *28*, 55
Hypericum 67

F

Ilex 17, 62
Impatiens 27, 71, *71*
inert growing media 27, *27*
internodal cuttings 28, *28*, *33*, 40
Iris 45
iron deficiency *59*

J K

Jasminum 67
Juniperus 63
Kalanchoe 42, 77
knives 24, *24*
  sterilizing 25, *25*

L

Laburnum 37, 62, *62*
Lamium 9
Lavandula 67, *67*
leaf-bud cuttings *29*, 40–41, *40–41*
leaf cuttings 9, *9*, *29*, 42–43, *42–43*
leaf mold, in media 26
leafless stem cuttings 46, *46*
Lewisia 72
Liquidambar 30, *30*
Lithops 77
loam 26
Lobelia 72, *72*
Lonicera 16, 40, 41, 67
Lupinus 72, *72*

M

Magnolia 16, 23, 32, 62, *63*
Mahonia 9, *29*, 40, 67
mallet cuttings 35, *35*
Mammillaria 21, 77
manganese deficiency *59*
media 26–27, *26*
Mentha 19, 72
meristem 13, 14
Metasequoia 37, *37*
micropropagation 13, *13*
mint *19*, 29, 45, 72
mist propagation 12, *13*, *51*, 56
Monarda 72, *72*
Morisia 75
Morus 62

N

Nicotiana 13
nodal cuttings *15*, 28, *28*, *33*, 40
Nothofagus 17
nursery beds 49, 58, *58*
Nymphaea 72

O

Oenothera 18, 72–73
Opuntia 77, *77*
Osteospermum 73
outdoor cuttings 58–59

P

Pachyphytum oviferum 42
Papaver 73
part-leaf cuttings *43*
Passiflora 40, 67
peat 26
peat blocks 27, *27*
Pelargonium 6, 73
Penstemon 27, 73, *73*
perennials 18–19, 23, 38–39, 69–75
perlite 26, 39, *39*
pests 55, *59*
Philadelphus 30, 67
Philodendron 40, 67
Phlox 38, 73, *73*

[R column start]

Picea 63
pinching out 57, *57*
pipings *19*, 34, *34*
Pittosporum 68
plastic film 12
Podocarpus 63, *63*
Populus 37
Potamogeton 73
pots 24, *24*, *25*
potting 57, *57*
powdery mildew *59*
preparing cuttings 28–29
Primula 19, 73–74, *73*
propagators *50*, *51*, 56
pruners 24, *24*
Prunus 30, 62–63
Pulsatilla 44
pumice 46
Pyracantha 28, 68, *68*

R

Ramonda 9
Rebutia 77
regeneration 14–15
Rhipsalis 77
rhizome cuttings 45, *45*
Rhododendron 68
Rhus typhina 44
Ribes 68
Robinia 63
rockwool 27, *27*
rooting media 26–27, *26–27*
roots:
  regeneration 14–15, *15*
  root cuttings 9, *9*, *29*, 44–45, *44–45*
  rooting times 40
Rosa 30, 68
rosemary 9, 29
rosette cuttings *29*, 46, *46*, *47*
Rubus cockburnianus 40
Rudbeckia 74, *74*

S

Saintpaulia 9, 42, *42*, 74
Salix 29, 63

Salvia 9, 29, 38, 68, 74
sand 26, 37, *37*
Sansevieria 29, 42, 74
Saxifraga 29, 75
Schlumbergera 47, 77, 77
Sedum 29, 77
semi-ripe cuttings 23, *29*, 32–35, *32–35*
Sempervivum 77
shading 54, *54*, *58*
sharpening stones *24*
shoots, ripening 28
shrubs 16, 23, 64–68
    hardwood cuttings 36
    leaf-bud cuttings 40–41
    semi-ripe cuttings 32
    softwood cuttings 30
slugs *59*
softwood cuttings 9, 23, *29*, 30–31, *30–31*
soil 27
soil-warming cables *51*
Solenostemon 9, 27, *27*, *57*, 74, *74*

stem cuttings 9, 23, *29*
    basal stem cuttings 29, 38–39, *38–39*
    cacti, 47, *47*
    leafless 46, *46*
    stem-tip cuttings 29
stem roots 14, *14–15*
stock plants 23, *23*, 38, *38*
Streptocarpus 9, *29*, 42, *43*, 75
succulents 20–1, 42, 46, 47, 76–77
suckers 44
Syringa 68

T

Taxus 27, 63
temperature 54, 57
Thymus 68
tools 24, *24*
transpiration 54
trays, cell 25, *25*
trees 16–17, 23, 36, 37, 61–63
trimming cuttings 28
tunnel cloches *52*

U V

Ulmus 30
vegetative propagation 8–9
ventilation 49, 54, *54*
Verbascum *74*, 75
vermiculite *26*
Viburnum 68
vine weevils *59*
Viola 39, 75
virus diseases *59*
Vitis 68, *68*

W Y

water, rooting in 27, *27*
water-retentive gel 27, *27*
watering 55, *55*, *59*
whitefly 55, *55*
widgers 24, *24*
wind protection *58*
Wisteria 68
woody plants 16–17
"wound" roots 14, *15*
Yucca *29*, 46, *46*, 68

ACKNOWLEDGMENTS

Picture Research Anna Grapes
DK Picture Library Romaine Werblow
Index Hilary Bird

Dorling Kindersley would like to thank:
All staff at the RHS, in particular Barbara Haynes, Simon Maughan, and Susanne Mitchell.

American Horticultural Society
To learn more about the work of the Society, visit AHS on the internet at www.ahs.org or call 1-800-777-7931.

Photography
The publisher would like to thank the following for their kind permission to reproduce their photographs:
(key: t=top, b=bottom, r=right, l=left, c=center, GPL=Garden Picture Library, MEPL= Mary Evans Picture Library, SPL=Science Photo Library)

2: GPL/Eric Crichton; **5:** GPL/Eric Crichton (bl); **6:** GPL/Paul Hart; **10:** MEPL; **11:** Peter Cross (r), GPL/John Glover (l); **13:** Holt/Nigel Cattlin (br), SPL/Sinclair Stammers (bc); **14:** GPL/Brian Carter (bl), SPL/Francoise Sauze (br); **17:** GPL/Lamontagne (bl, br), GPL/Ron Evans (tr); **19:** John Fielding (tl), GPL/Eric Crichton (b), GPL/J S Sira (tr), GPL/John Glover (c); **21:** GPL/J S Sira (t); **22:** Harry Smith; **48:** Holt/Rosie Mayer; **50:** Photos Horticultural (cl); **53:** GPL/Mel Watson (tl), GPL/Michael Howes (tr); **55:** Holt/Nigel Cattlin (bl), SPL/James King-Holmes (bc), Harry Smith (br); **59:** GPL/Vaughan Fleming (bl); Holt/Alan & Linda Detrick (br), Holt/Nigel Cattlin (cl, c, bc); **60:** GPL/Mayer/Le Scanff; **62:** GPL/Robert Estall (bc).

All other images © Dorling Kindersley.
For further information see:
www.dkimages.com